Urban Gardens

Urban Gardens

PLANS AND PLANTING DESIGNS

Ann-Marie Powell

Specially commissioned photography
by Steven Wooster

CASSELL ILLUSTRATED

To Jules and our new baby

First published in Great Britain in 2005 by Cassell Illustrated,
a division of Octopus Publishing Group Limited
2–4 Heron Quays, London E14 4JP

Distributed in the United States of America by
Sterling Publishing Co., Inc.,
387 Park Avenue South, New York, NY 10016-8810

A CIP catalogue record for this book is available from the British Library.

ISBN 1 8440 3153 5
EAN 9781844031535

This book produced by R & R Publishing
Pippa Rubinstein & Judith Robertson

Printed in China

CONTENTS

Climate zones

Suitable climate zones are included for the plants used in this book. As a simple guide, the UK, lowland France and Germany, and East and West Coast United States, fall into zones 8 and 9 and all plants in this book should grow there. Northern USA, the Rockies, Canada and Eastern Europe are in zones 3–5.

INTRODUCTION

Shoehorned into the smallest patches of ground, tacked to the rear, side and even precariously on the roof of homes that are themselves squeezed between factory, tower block or in row upon row of tightly packed buildings, precious urban gardens are increasingly contributing to the greening of the city. Today, they have never been more popular. With the ever-increasing pace of urban living and its long working days, gardens provide the ideal antidote to a hectic day rushing around the city.

Urban gardens have a relaxing quality that soothes us once off the busy pavement and behind our own front door. They are a uniquely personal vision of the owner's idea of Eden, and form a living, dynamic canvas of ever-changing leaf, flower, colour and scent. The town garden has come into its own as the grounding mechanism that city dwellers are looking for, and the therapeutic benefits to be gained from nurturing and caring for a garden should not be underestimated. Whether a balcony, roof terrace or small back yard, the value of a personal outdoor space in which to relax and unwind has never been higher. The town garden is now an essential part of urban living.

Although they may initially seem vast in the small garden, oversized beds allow for a deep layering of planting that will look good throughout the seasons.

The small size of most urban gardens makes them exciting places to be; small spaces have to be developed with imagination to ensure that every scrap of space is utilized. Just as country gardens work best when they echo their local environment and draw from surrounding materials and plants, city spaces are most successful when they do the same. However, urban gardeners have a much wider palette to choose from. The diversity of the city, with its blend of people, cultures, architecture, noise, colours and multitude of materials, cuts the urban gardener loose from the need to conform to the conventional idea of the garden. You can afford to be brave, eclectic and individual, creating whatever you like, so that your garden becomes a reflection of you and your character against the background of the city. No matter how you choose to adorn it or what you decide to grow, be your final choices quietly conservative or avant garde, your garden needs to look at home in the urban environment.

But where to begin? You will need to mix practicality and aesthetics to create that valued extra living space, and the best place to start is to think of your plot of land as a continuation of the rooms within your home. Just as you would with a room indoors, think about style, colour, mood and practical considerations of storage, seating, budget and maintenance. For the majority of us, budget will be key. Though urban 'outdoor rooms' often bring to mind high-tech, hard-edged minimalist spaces adorned with a few low-maintenance specimen

plants, they don't have to be so. Slick contemporary style needs a considerable investment of cash, running to the expense of skilled construction and mature specimen plants, making this option a luxury that few but the most affluent or highly skilled home improvers can afford. Many city gardens are eclectic spaces brimming with prized trees, fruit, perennials and vegetables, all vying for attention. With a small area, the urban gardener has to be imaginative when planting, while at the same time considering maintenance issues if there will be a limited amount of time available to spend looking after the space. Consider also what you want to use the space for; a young, growing family may need to be accommodated, the strong architecture of a house supported, friends entertained and ultimately dreams realized.

The range of choices available can itself be bewildering. Often, the biggest hurdle to overcome when furnishing an urban space is committing to any one scheme. Although rules are made to be broken, particularly in town gardens, it is a good idea to begin with a strong theme and develop it gradually, rather than dabbling with a collection of half-hearted attempts that end up forming a visual blur. Each of the ten gardens in this book began with a single idea given by the clients themselves (though sometimes without their realizing). I hope that these gardens will spark ideas in your own mind, or provide you with the confidence to develop your own garden, even if it is your first.

Every garden discussed in this book includes a plan, planting guide and details on how and why the garden was approached in a certain way. The needs of the client are examined, and the solutions to a variety of problems are explored. Where appropriate, certain site considerations are discussed, from soil type and aspect to the views and vistas that needed to be screened or emphasized.

Approaching your garden in a similar way, before you begin planting, will help you understand its strengths and weaknesses. Get to know your garden really well by simply spending time in it. Start by assessing its soil type and determining which direction is south (the area of the garden that faces south will receive the most light and, of course, heat), then consider the views that you may like to accentuate or block out altogether and the different levels within the space if it is not flat, measuring and plotting these and other existing features on paper as you go. Once you are thoroughly familiar with your garden's current features, you can begin to decide what to change and add. Should you put a terrace in sun or shade? Would you like to maximize growing opportunities with a pergola, gazebo or arbour? Perhaps a water feature would block out the city's sounds? Where should a shed be sited should you require one, and how will you be led around the space in order to make the best use of even the most diminutive garden? Even if you employ a garden designer, working out your needs and desires first will help him or her to design a space that works for you.

Ultimately, this research will help you create a space that you feel comfortable within and are proud of, but once your garden is built, remember that it will need help from yourself if it is to continue to develop and look good. A season-by-season maintenance guide at the end of this book will help you to look after and improve your space as it matures and grows; nurturing your plants is not only good for the garden but, after a particularly heavy week, can save your sanity, too. Believe me, pottering is bliss!

So before you decide to tarmac that little patch of earth next to your house, studio or flat to provide an extra parking space, consider how much your own urban Eden would add to the quality of your life, not to mention the price of your property. I hope this book will give you some ideas.

Use your urban garden not only as an extension of your home, but also as an extension of your personality. In town, anything goes – you can make your garden calm and serene, or as dramatic as you like.

URBAN OASIS

Enclosed within a cool rendered boundary, tiers of plants, an elegant rill and a host of terraces combine to form a green, serene space with timeless modernity. Changes in levels and jostling plants create varying vistas of interest no matter where you stand, sit or perch within this garden. A raised bed at the rear forms a stage from which the plants perform. Water plants jostle in and beside a rill that falls from the main planting bed to the garden's floor, maximizing planting opportunities. With a strong but simple design, the garden makes the most of the space, with plants highlighting the seasons as they change.

PLANNING the GARDEN

Both clients here had a great love of gardening and knew they would be spending most of their summers within the space, but unfortunately the garden was overlooked on every side, denying privacy on any level. Some kind of screening was therefore essential if they were to enjoy their garden without feeling ill at ease within it.

With a newly developed interior in the house, it was important that the garden also had a strong identity. It had to be elegant, stylish and modern, but not be quick to date. A variety of functions was expected of the space, too. A highly sociable household, the space had to be large enough to accommodate a number of guests without losing its personal feel, but had to retain areas in which to read the newspaper and relax privately in peace. Although by many standards the overall size is small, in an urban environment the ground area is actually reasonably large. After years of cramped gardening, cooped up within tiny spaces, the clients were keen to create the garden of their dreams; it was a pleasure to be the facilitator.

The garden had to deliver in other areas, too. Attached to a house with several storeys and rooms on many levels, the garden would be viewed from the conservatory and the French windows of the living room as well as from above.

Even though the plants were to be a focus here, a strong design was required to make the space work as a whole. Many plant-biased gardens successfully use curves to echo the natural shapes and informal lines found within nature, but in this town garden, straight lines forming interlocking shapes create a stronger sense of belonging, especially when seen from above. Interlocking shapes reflected in the

Water can be incorporated into even the smallest garden, allowing a whole new sphere of planting.

surrounding urban environment help to integrate the garden into its surroundings. The clients' great love of plants would be obvious in the garden's detail, with strong foliage and flower shapes crammed into overflowing beds to soften any harsh straight planes or uncomfortably sharp angles.

The garden would also be in full view from the conservatory at ground level. I therefore decided to create layers of planting, with beds viewed through beds, reaching a crescendo at the rear. Evergreen pieces would form year-round interest but would also pull the eye through, around and up into the rear space to create the illusion that the garden was much bigger than it really was.

A spectacular focal point was called for outside the French windows and we decided on a water feature that would seemingly advance towards you. Dropping from one level to another, a split rill would create noise and movement, courting attention from within the house. This rill, or long channel of water, would also break the garden into separate areas.

Varying levels would add to a sense of journey and break up the singular flat plane that so many gardens are built upon. Different materials used in each surface level would emphasize these level changes. Indeed, a simple level change can create more interest than even a bed of unusual plants.

Finally, if we were to achieve anything green, the earth would require attention. Years of building rubble had been thrown into the garden and the existing soil was suffering from neglect. The owners were keen to grow a wide range of plants, so it was paramount that this issue be dealt with as soon as possible and the soil vastly improved.

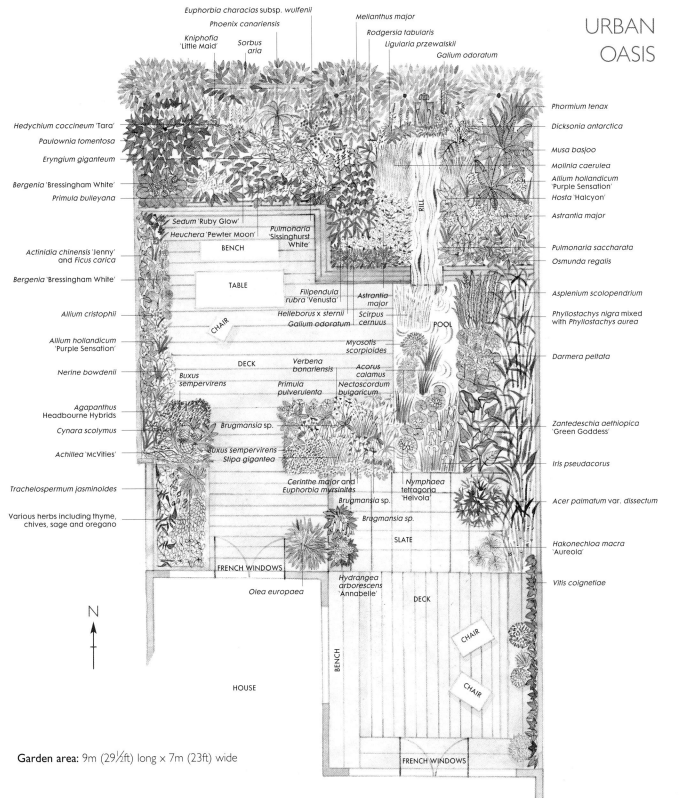

Euphorbia characias subsp. wulfenii
Phoenix canariensis
Kniphofia 'Little Maid'
Sorbus aria
Melianthus major
Rodgersia tabularis
Ligularia przewalskii
Galium odoratum

Hedychium coccineum 'Tara'
Paulownia tomentosa
Eryngium giganteum
Bergenia 'Bressingham White'
Primula bulleyana

Phormium tenax
Dicksonia antarctica
Musa basjoo
Molinia caerulea
Allium hollandicum 'Purple Sensation'
Hosta 'Halcyon'
Astrantia major

Sedum 'Ruby Glow'
Heuchera 'Pewter Moon'
Pulmonaria 'Sissinghurst White'

BENCH

Actinidia chinensis 'Jenny' and Ficus carica
Bergenia 'Bressingham White'

TABLE

Pulmonaria saccharata
Osmunda regalis

Filipendula rubra 'Venusta'
Astrantia major
Helleborus x sternii
Scirpus cernuus
Galium odoratum

RILL

Asplenium scolopendrium

Allium cristophii

CHAIR

POOL

Phyllostachys nigra mixed with Phyllostachys aurea

Allium hollandicum 'Purple Sensation'

Myosotis scorpioides

Darmera peltata

Nerine bowdenii

DECK

Verbena bonariensis

Acorus calamus

Buxus sempervirens

Primula pulverulenta
Nectoscordum bulgaricum

Agapanthus Headbourne Hybrids
Cynara scolymus

Brugmansia sp.

Zantedeschia aethiopica 'Green Goddess'

Achillea 'McVities'

Buxus sempervirens
Stipa gigantea

Iris pseudacorus

Trachelospermum jasminoides

Cerinthe major and Euphorbia myrsinites

Nymphaea tetragona 'Helvola'

Acer palmatum var. dissectum

Various herbs including thyme, chives, sage and oregano

Brugmansia sp.
Brugmansia sp.

SLATE

Hakonechloa macra 'Aureola'

FRENCH WINDOWS

Hydrangea arborescens 'Annabelle'

Vitis coignetiae

Olea europaea

DECK

N

CHAIR

HOUSE

BENCH

CHAIR

Garden area: 9m (29½ft) long x 7m (23ft) wide

FRENCH WINDOWS

SPECIAL FEATURES

A ll the special features in the garden needed to work together in order to lead the user logically around the space. A finely balanced juggling act and a strict approach to space and proportion ensured success through changes in material, colours and heights.

Rill

Formalized manmade water courses, or rills, not only add movement to the urban space, but depending upon your mood and the design of the water course chosen, also add excitement or an air of relaxation. The rill in this garden acted as a focal point, incorporating a waterfall to increase its impact. In essence, the rill was built as two separate ponds, one section within the raised bed elevated above a second pool at ground level. A fall stone (carefully positioned so that water did not fall against the rendered wall) was situated at the end of the higher pool, allowing water to fall as a sheet into the lower pond when the power was switched on. A submersible pump powers this feat, stationed within a purposely deeper portion of the lower pool. When switched on, the pump forces excess water up a pipe into the rear of the upper pond, circulating water evenly and effectively and negating the risk of overflow when the pump is switched off. Constructed in concrete for longevity (though you could form yours from a flexible liner), the pool's walls were painted with black water sealant in order to camouflage the pump and create the illusion of depth in what is essentially only a shallow body of water.

Changes in level give the garden greater visual appeal. This is enhanced by a waterfall that adds sound, movement and drama to the effect.

Surfaces

Two large decks outside the main viewing areas from the house formed the majority of the garden's surface area. This linked the vistas together, but each deck fulfilled a distinctly different function. The deck within the garden proper formed the main terrace for entertaining, being perfectly suited due to its size, the amount of sunlight available and its proximity to the kitchen. This area encompassed a large table, with additional seating provided by timber capping on the rendered wall around the raised bed, creating the perfect place to stop and perch for a quick chat.

Above The different building materials are linked by their complementary colours and tones, and held together with contrasting textures of green foliage.

Right Leaves add interest to the garden long after its flowers have faded. Place different leaf shapes next to each other to ensure a long season of interest.

The secondary deck outside the living area's main windows was kept reasonably clear so that it did not detract from the main feature, the rill. Built-in benches along the walls joined the rill at a right angle, providing impromptu seating that would not clutter the space.

The two decks were divided by a lower section of slate, a darker material that linked with the edging used in the rill, but separated the decks.

Raised bed

Though highly designed, this space was certainly a gardener's garden and it was essential that a large border be incorporated within it to accommodate a depth of planting. Whether raised or not, never be too mean with the width of planting beds when creating them; the wider the border, the greater the number of plants you have space to grow. More plants can be accommodated in wider beds, allowing you to create a changing picture in your garden with blooms following blooms, essentially increasing the season of interest in your planting.

It was decided to create a raised bed in this garden to highlight the importance of plants. On a more practical note, the raised bed also made plants easier to maintain, added interest to the space and enabled us to provide the best growing medium possible with newly conditioned, weed-free, fertile soil. At over 2m (6ft 6in) wide and with this imported quality soil, our planting opportunities were certainly maximized.

Lighting extends the interest of your garden after dark, creating whole new scenes as the light grazes through a space, highlighting details and plants that may not be so obvious during daylight hours. These new vistas can be enjoyed while you are within the space or viewing it from indoors.

Trellis

Instead of using the usual trellising available from every garden centre, we decided to create an unusual bespoke 'wrap' for the garden with horizontal lengths of timber. These trellises would not only raise the height atop the rendered walls of the garden's boundaries, thereby increasing the space's privacy, but would also become a garden feature that increased the boundary's aesthetic value. It was attached with metal brackets mechanically bolted into the top of the wall to provide fixing points to which lengths of timber were screwed. The horizontal lengths of timber were uniform in depth but varied in width, and became an important ornamental detail in the space.

Light

Electrics were added to the garden to power the water pump, so it seemed wasteful not to add some elementary lighting to the scheme. A few electric lights were added primarily to planting beds in order to add depth and a changing background scene that could be enjoyed when looking out from the house after dark. This technique makes window glass seemingly disappear, so that the window frame appears to frame a picture of the garden. Enhanced by the ever-charming ambience of candles, the lights bring the garden alive after dark, thereby extending the hours in which it can be enjoyed.

If your budget does not stretch to electric lighting, candlelight can be used just as effectively. Scattered around a garden, night lights offer an inviting gentle twinkle, warm up walls with their gentle glow and encourage interesting shadows.

PLANTS and PLANTING

In order to provide interest all year round, well-stocked borders formed a wide and varied planting arrangement. As keen gardeners, my clients were eager to incorporate as many unusual varieties as possible through every range of plants. Aquatics, marginals, herbaceous perennials and shrubs were considered and the planting even included a pleached *Sorbus aria* aerial hedge at the rear of the garden to form an unusual living screen.

A deep and generous raised planting bed at the rear of the space allowed us to incorporate our own mix of moist, fertile soil, the perfect medium in which to grow an array of plants. The length of this planting space and its width allowed us to layer plants behind each other so there would always be something to look at no matter what time of year it was.

Shrubs are not the only plants that give evergreen interest to the garden. *Helleborus* x *sternii* forms a groundcover of attractive leathery leaves and beautifully delicate winter flowers.

Astrantia major is a fabulous late summer bloomer, useful for extending the season of interest in your borders up until the first frosts.

Helleborus **x** *sternii* (zones 6–9) is a very useful plant because it flowers when little else is happening in the garden. It is a fabulously attractive member of the hellebore family with its rosy, glaucous-green foliage, each leaf composed of three leaflets held aloft upon pinkish purple stems. Late winter to mid-spring gives rise to creamy green flower, often flushed pink, that measure 2.5–5cm (1–2in) across. Remove any dead, damaged or diseased foliage while the plant is flowering to promote new growth and accentuate the blooms. Provide your plant with moist, fertile, neutral to alkaline soil in full sun or dappled shade and in maturity your plants will reach roughly 35cm (14in) high.

Astrantia major (zones 4–7) has delicate but insignificant flowers, with its attraction lying in the ruff-like collars within which the true flower nestles. The lobed, palmate leaves are also a useful addition to the border, forming a good all-round plant that associates well with a host of other plants and flowers freely. Indeed you may find astrantia a little too free and easy as it self-seeds prolifically. Simply pull up excess plants. *A. major* does well in woodland gardens, on stream banks and in moist borders where it will reach a height of 90cm (36in) and spread to a width of 45cm (18in).

At the water's edge, large, heart-shaped leaves give rise to the otherworldly flowers of *Zantedeschia aethiopica* 'Green Goddess' in late spring and early summer.

Large balls of metallic pink-purple flowers held upon stiff stems make *Allium cristophii* an exceptional summer-flowering bulb.

Shrubs give a garden structure and, whether grown in the border or in a large container, deciduous *Hydrandea arborescens* 'Annabelle' gives considerable impact all summer.

Zantedeschia aethiopica '**Green goddess**' (zones 8–10) is commonly known as an arum lily and has a green-white flower that is in fact a modified leaf, botanically named a 'spathe', that encircles the central spike. It adds a cool, serene air to any water feature, though it is equally happy on land as it is in the water. Do bear in mind that the arum lily is not reliably hardy in all but the warmest areas. If you would like more obviously white spathes than *Z.a.* 'Green Goddess', seek out *Z.a.* 'Crowborough'. Both reach a height of 90cm (36in) and spread of 60cm (24in). Take care when handling these plants because their sap can be a painful skin irritant.

Allium cristophii (zones 3–7) is wonderfully architectural. To achieve the best results, plant the bulbs in groups in autumn, with each bulb at a depth of 5–10cm (2–4in) in well-drained soil in a sunny position. Each bulb will give rise to a large, symmetrical umbel reaching 15–20cm (6–8in) in diameter. The umbel is composed of dozens of star-shaped flowers held upon a stiff 45cm (18in) tall stem. When they have finished flowering, the flowers dry out to form valuable seed heads, opening to reveal shiny black seeds in winter.

Hydrangea arborescens '**Annabelle**' (zones 3–9) has huge clusters of flowers up to 25cm (10in) across that open green in summer, quickly developing with age into a sumptuous creamy white. This is a wonderfully adaptable plant, and provided it is given moist, fertile soil, it will grow in acid or alkaline ground and in full sun or deep shade; every gardener can successfully grow this plant. Do not deadhead the blooms; instead allow flowers to drop away naturally. This is because the new flower bud that will flower the following year is produced just behind the old flower bud and, in removing the old, you could damage the new. Ultimate height and spread is 2.5 × 2.5m (8 × 8ft).

The elegant, gently weeping habit of *Hakonechloa macra* 'Aureola' makes it the perfect subject for a container on your terrace.

With its huge leaves, fibrous trunk and immense size, it is easy to see how the exotic good looks of the tree fern, *Dicksonia antarctica*, have captured the imaginations of so many gardeners.

Some culinary plants are so ornamental that they fit seamlessly into a decorative planting border. Globe artichoke (*Cynara scolymus*) is a wonderful perennial vegetable addition to any jungle border.

Hakonechloa macra 'Aureola' (zones 4–9) originates from the mountainous areas of Japan. This slow-growing grass gradually forms a dense carpet of foliage when planted at ground level, but can look more impressive when planted in a pot. The brightly variegated leaves in lime and emerald green assume a pink tint in autumn, turning reddish purple as the season progresses. In the open ground, grow this plant in fertile moist soil in full sun or partial shade to form a 15–25cm (6–10in) high mound with an eventual spread of 40cm (16in). If you prefer to grow it in a pot, use a good all-purpose compost and water and feed regularly.

Dicksonia antarctica (zones 9–11) is the largest of the dicksonias. It has been known to reach an incredible 18m (50ft) in height, but a mature height of around 6m (20ft) is more usual. Large fronds grow to about 3m (10ft) in length, and each plant's crown contains several fronds; up to 60 or 70 have been noted on one plant. Position it as near to its natural surroundings as possible; under the shade of a tree with some direct sunlight and in humus-rich soil. An acid soil is preferred, too. Apply a high-nitrogen feed once a month during the growing season and water the plant at the crown rather than the base of the trunk. Fill the crown to overflowing during hot spells, letting water pour down the trunk, and in winter protect the crown from frost using either its own old fronds or straw.

Cynara scolymus (zones 8–10) reaches a magnificent 2m (6ft) in height and has few visual differences from its more usually planted ornamental cousin, *C. cardunculus*. The primary difference is in taste and in which parts of the plant are harvested. Though the leaf-stalks and mid-ribs of *C. cardunculus* can be eaten, the flower-heads are usually left on the plant. However, *C. scolymus* has been bred to produce tasty flower-heads that are harvested in bud, while still immature. *C. scolymus* requires a sheltered sunny spot in order to do well, in rich, well-draining soil. It is an easy-to-grow plant that requires little maintenance. Water plants well in summer and protect them in autumn, particularly if your garden is prone to harsh winter weather. Replace every three years or so to maintain peak levels of productivity.

Large sword-like leaves, each measuring up to 3m (10ft) long, rise in massed peaks from the ground to make *Phormium tenax* king of the plants when it comes to architectural drama.

With massed layers of delicate foliage, *Acer palmatum* var. *dissectum* forms an eye-catching display throughout the summer, with a final fanfare of vivid autumn colour.

Melianthus major is a desirable foliage plant that looks good in an exotic garden or border, particularly when underplanted with hedychiums, cannas or bananas.

Phormium tenax (zones 9–11), commonly known as New Zealand flax, is a useful plant in tropical gardens but also when providing punctuation in cottage or meadow planting schemes. Rigid, leathery green uprights bulk up with time to form substantial clumps measuring up to 2m (6ft) wide. Otherworldly flower-spikes of bronze-red are produced in summer on plants aged over three to four years old, reaching an amazing 4m (13ft) in height. Phormiums detest any kind of waterlogging, preferring open soil in full sun, but will tolerate high degrees of pollution, making them the perfect plant for urban gardens and areas along the coast.

Acer palmatum var. *dissectum* (zones 5–8) is a plant so charming that almost everyone falls in love with it. Very dissected leaves unfold light green in spring, turning a red-green in summer, firing up to brilliant orange in autumn. This display is certainly enthralling, so give it centre stage. Use this plant as a feature shrub or in a large container at the edge of a terrace. In the open ground this acer prefers neutral to acid soil, but tolerates very alkaline soil if kept well watered. Make sure you site your plant in an area of dappled shade because harsh summer sun will scorch the foliage, potentially causing serious damage to your plant, as will a late frost. Cover the plant with a sheet of horticultural fleece if you think it may be at risk. The ultimate mature height of this slow-growing shrub is 2 x 3m (6 x 10ft).

Melianthus major (zones 9–10) is grown for its attractive grey-green foliage. Though at first glance each arching branch looks like a single leaf, these metallic green spreading branches are composed of several leaflets that together form a whole. Given its preferred conditions of fertile, moist, well-drained soil in full sun, *M. major* will reach an ultimate height of 2–3m (6–10ft), though this is unusual. Originating from South Africa, *M. major* is only marginally hardy, just surviving temperatures of slightly below 0°C (32°F), and only then if the plant has developed well over a particularly good summer. In order to protect this plant from winter's freezing temperatures, it is therefore essential to give it a deep dry winter mulch and protection from excessive winter wet.

MODERN URBAN HARDSCAPE

Bold, confident and undoubtedly urban, this garden embraces hard rather than soft landscaping in order to reflect the urban environment that surrounds it. Materials brazenly take the lead, creating a slick inventive space with the focus on aesthetics. Modern hard landscaping techniques are utilized to create an architectural, evenly proportioned space, the scales tipped unashamedly towards its structure, its clean lines and properties of low, low maintenance. The clients were unafraid of strong colour, so planes of brightly painted surface were incorporated to wow visitors. Colour emphasizes the elegant, uncomplicated nature of the space, drawing all the elements together to form the essence of today's modern patio living.

PLANNING the GARDEN

Whatever the weather, no matter the time of day or season, this garden had to have impact. Within the urban environment, surrounded by so much architectural 'noise', the garden can be unrestrained, taking its inspiration from anywhere. With such a plethora of material choices available, a garden can be whatever you want it to be, but confined patches of outdoor space need to be carefully utilized to their full potential. Owners of small urban gardens understandably want to stamp their personalities onto their space, claiming the land as their own. This gives rise to experimentation and creativity as people mix practicality and aesthetics in the tiniest areas. Cities allow the gardener a degree of inventiveness that would look out of place in the country.

I wanted to create a visual feast in this postage-stamp size plot that measured only 8 x 4.5m (26 x 13½ft), taking my inspiration from the light industry and spread of townhouses that sprawled around the neighbourhood and overlooked this garden from every side.

In essence, this garden would be divided into three sections, each separated by rendered walls at different levels, each chunk with its own personality and its own function. The divided sections would combine aesthetics, function and form that, when seen together, would make a coherent whole.

The first section, leading from the house, needed to introduce the garden to the viewer situated in the living room, or anybody stepping out into the garden for the first time. Though the design was modern, it was important that every sensory experience be maximized,

Large swathes of vibrant colour painted on rendered walls creates a surprisingly soft backdrop against which to enjoy plants.

so at the client's request a small square of lawn led from the first section of garden into the second – perfect for those barefoot moments. A small corridor would funnel them out into the space, the hard lines edged with boldly flowering and scented plants to blur the hard landscaping. These plants edging the garden's floor would soften the area, firmly establishing the space as a garden. The addition of a folding table and chairs in this section made it an intimate space close to the house where one could sit and read the paper with a cup of coffee while enjoying the view just beyond, which would constantly change as sunlight played upon bold surfaces of soft purple colour on the rendered walls.

The second and central area was to be set aside completely for socializing. Though the space was small, a large seating area was to be included, and the floor space needed to be large enough to accommodate summer parties and barbecues. Lots of people walking through this tiny space might do untold damage to plants at ground level, so only raised beds were used to to ensure that plants would be out of reach. This was to be a functional, funky, sociable space for enjoying with friends.

The rear of the garden was to be the utility area. On a practical level, storage had to be incorporated somewhere but we did not want it to be seen, and with the use of some kind of screen this area would be visually blocked out to provide a false end to the garden and a visual full stop. Bamboo was planted at the very rear of the space to trick the eye into thinking the garden carried on beyond the boundary.

MODERN URBAN HARDSCAPE

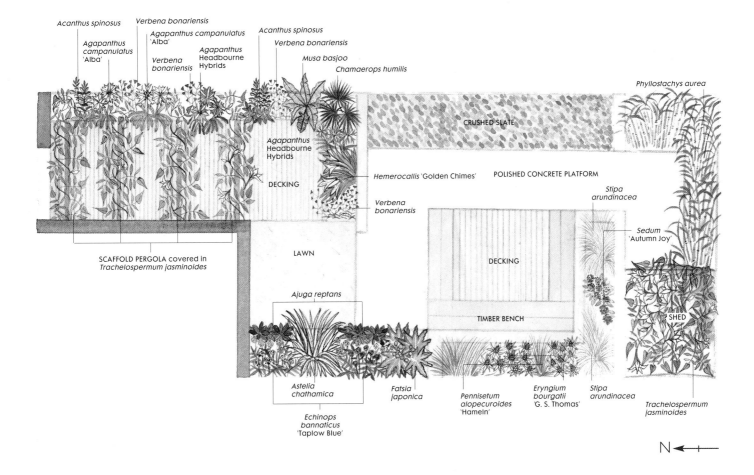

Acanthus spinosus

Agapanthus campanulatus 'Alba'

Verbena bonariensis

Agapanthus campanulatus 'Alba'

Verbena bonariensis

Agapanthus Headbourne Hybrids

Acanthus spinosus

Verbena bonariensis

Musa basjoo

Chamaerops humilis

Phyllostachys aurea

CRUSHED SLATE

Agapanthus Headbourne Hybrids

DECKING

POLISHED CONCRETE PLATFORM

Hemerocallis 'Golden Chimes'

Stipa arundinacea

Verbena bonariensis

Sedum 'Autumn Joy'

SCAFFOLD PERGOLA covered in Trachelospermum jasminoides

LAWN

DECKING

Ajuga reptans

TIMBER BENCH

SHED

Astelia chathamica

Fatsia japonica

Pennisetum alopecuroides 'Hameln'

Eryngium bourgatii 'G. S. Thomas'

Stipa arundinacea

Trachelospermum jasminoides

Echinops bannaticus 'Taplow Blue'

N ⟵—

Garden area: 5m (16½ft) long x 8m (26ft) wide

SPECIAL FEATURES

Though small, this garden would be perfectly formed, creating a minimalist space made up of pared-down shapes and structures. Though at first glance these strong blocks seemingly glide through the garden, they are visually connected with sheets of colour to create a blended whole. Taking the lead from bold walls of colour within the house as well as inspiration from the immediate surroundings, this garden was to be a firmly urban landscape while at the same time creating respite from the unrelenting pace of city living. To create a feeling of intimacy, we surrounded the garden with lightly coloured boundaries that would enclose the space. These boundaries were made from sheets of marine plywood painted light cream to reflect light and to keep the occupants' attentions inside the garden.

Rendered walls

We needed to maximize the feeling of space, so it was important to create some kind of journey through the garden to expand its horizons. To achieve this, we decided to split the garden into sections through implied division with some sort of screening. Suggested division in this way allows glimpses of what lies beyond the immediate space, creating intrigue and curiosity. By encouraging the desire to investigate further and to explore, and providing lots to look at as they travel, users can be fooled into thinking the area is larger than it really is.

A scaffold pole pergola echoes the urban landscape and will act as a support for climbers, adding a visual lift to the space.

Rendered walls increasing in height from front to back provided the perfect solution. It was important to create as much interest as possible and, though the walls would be unified by painting them the same colour, they would each have different functions.

The first wall (and the shortest) was placed as a semi-screen that one could see over, but prevented the whole garden from being seen in one go on first stepping outside. Situated at the end of a long length of decking, on which there were folding table and chairs, this wall also formed the backdrop to an informal seating area and plants.

Of course, this first wall could also be viewed and utilized within the second section of the garden. The second section was the largest area, ideal for a gathering of family and friends. The height of the wall made it perfect for leaning against or stowing glasses and bottles of wine.

The second wall formed a backrest to the timber bench but its primary function was as a large raised planter. Intermediate in height between the front and rear internal walls, this raised planter elevated plants to a height where they could be admired, but kept them out of harm's way behind a bench in case a party started getting boisterous.

The final wall created a false ending to the garden, with an opening at one side allowing access to a shed behind it. Bamboo sited directly behind this opening at the rear of the garden created a vista down the whole length of the garden.

The rich, vibrant purple tones (exterior masonry paint was used for its weatherproof properties) linked the walls together to unify the space but

Strong horizontal and vertical lines in the hard landscaping are softened by sweeps of planting at varying heights.

also gave the walls an ever-changing sculptural appeal. As the sun moves around the space, so do the tones of colour. Shadows are cast to form movement through a continually changing picture of colour and tone.

Concrete platform

Much maligned and definitely underused, concrete is an ideal material for the modern urban space. With any number of surface finishes, available in a variety of colours and easily formed into any shape, concrete is affordable, durable and effective. I chose to use it here, without joints, to form a seemingly floating solid platform snaking through the garden slightly above the overall ground height. The surface was polished to give it a glassy, sophisticated finish in direct contrast to the adjoining natural materials of timber and chipped slate. This highlighted the fact that at the heart of the garden lay a material that was gloriously manmade, again echoing and celebrating all that surrounded the space.

Seating

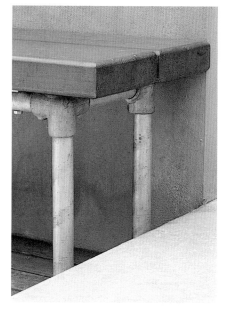

A large bench in the central segment of the garden was built from chunky pieces of timber to form a seating area – a compulsory feature in any garden. The purposeful lack of planting at ground level meant that any area within this section could be walked upon. The concrete path, raised in order to glide elegantly through the space, would also double to form further impromptu seating.

The bench was positioned so that it was backed on two sides by the medium-height rendered wall in order to form a backrest against the raised planting. One side was left open to prevent the area from becoming too enclosed and so that people could sit there without feeling restricted. This treatment was highly successful, optimizing space for as many people in the area as possible.

In order to strike a harmonious note with other materials used in the garden as well as add to the industrial theme, I used scaffolding to form the legs of the bench. Poles and joints were built to form a frame, then the timber seat fixed on top.

Slate shale is a great mulch for awkward areas.

Industrial fittings such as scaffold poles look great in the environment of the urban garden.

Slate shale border

Socializing was the primary function of the central section of this small garden, so any plants at ground level were likely to be damaged. I decided to keep the area plant-free but wanted it to have an attractive surface finish that could be trampled on without worry. Slate shale was chosen for this purpose. Fitting in with the tonal qualities of the painted, rendered walls and contrasting well with the strong form of the concrete, slate shale proved the perfect durable solution. The area was prepared with a thin layer of hardcore to provide a light foundation, then covered with a layer of weed-proof membrane. Finally, a 5–7.5cm (2–3in) deep layer of slate shale was poured on top.

The central area of the garden intended for socializing is kept clear and uncluttered, with the choice of materials and changes in level providing the primary visual interest.

PLANTS and PLANTING

Commonly, bold architectural plants such as palms, box balls and tropical plants are used in conjunction with modern minimalist gardens to emphasize the structural theme, and while I wanted to include such plants to anchor the planting to the space, I also wanted to include some softer-looking specimens to take the edge off so many hard lines in the landscaping.

A mixture of carefully selected evergreen shrubs and bamboo, herbaceous perennials and grasses would add rhythm, movement and scent to the space over the long summer period, while retaining a strong outline in winter. All of the selected plants were low maintenance and would pretty much look after themselves while the owners relaxed after a hard day's work in the city and simply enjoyed them.

Fatsia japonica's large glossy leaves of deepest green bounce light from the shadiest depths and can be relied upon all year round.

Snowballs of white blooms ensure that *Agapanthus campanulatus* 'Alba' is the centre of attention.

Fatsia japonica (zones 8–10) is a large evergreen shrub that provides year-round structure in the garden. *F. japonica* transforms shade from a difficult-to-plant area into a central focal point. Autumn brings otherworldly beads of blooms followed by clusters of black berries. Grow it in well-drained but moist, fertile soil, and water and feed regularly to encourage this plant to reach its ultimate height and spread of up to 3m (10ft).

Agapanthus campanulatus 'Alba' (zones 8–11) is an excellent border or container plant. Elegant strap-like leaves give rise to balls of blooms held high upon long strong stems in mid- to late summer. Hailing from South Africa, this plant is surprisingly hardy, though it may take a couple of seasons to bulk up and flower freely. Outside it enjoys a rich, light, well-drained soil, reaching an ultimate height of 90cm (36in). It also makes excellent cut flowers. It is perfect for growing in a container, and often blooms best when its roots are pot-bound. Plant the rhizomes so the top is 1cm (½in) below the soil's surface. Keep the soil moist and fertilize regularly throughout the season, if you do not use a slow-release fertilizer. In the autumn, in particularly cold areas, container-grown plants should be quickly moved to a bright frost-free location until the following spring.

Changing colour as the season progresses, *Stipa arundinacea's* outstanding shaggy texture softens even the hardest of structures. Its soft, wafting habit looks at home in gravel gardens, pots and beside paths – in fact, just about anywhere. This is a truly must-have plant.

Held high on thin spiny stems that defy gravity with their weight-lifting feats, *Verbena bonariensis* forms an elegant sculptural study in its own right when framed against the cream walls of this garden.

Stipa arundinacea (zones 8–11) earns its keep in the small urban garden, contributing much to a planting scheme. Although grasses do not offer brightly coloured flowers or architecturally bold foliage, they provide invaluable texture through their subtle shape, translucency and movement, catching even the slightest breath of a breeze. They are also extraordinarily easy to grow: drought-resistant, undemanding in their choice of soil conditions, requiring only sun to do well and little long-term maintenance. *S. arundinacea* is a New Zealand native that has all the best attributes of grasses and more besides. Amazingly soft

in appearance, *S. arundinacea* is something of a chameleon. New leaves appear chocolate brown, becoming olive green stained with rust, increasing in intensity after producing light sprays of golden inflorescence in the way of flower. The autumn display of yellows, reds and oranges becomes a major contribution to the garden, and the whole plant looks beautiful dusted with frost in winter. After a few years, plants may become a little threadbare but should have produced lots of offspring with which to replace the aged parent plants. The ultimate height and spread of this gorgeous grass is 45cm (18in).

Verbena bonariensis (zones 7–10) has tightly packed heads of violet flowers that seem to keep coming all summer long. It is a spindly plant, but grows tall, reaching heights of 1.5m (5ft). *En masse* it is strikingly architectural, and due to its self-seeding tendencies, it will not take long for plants to bulk up. A generous sprinkling of *V. bonariensis* will lift the spirits of any garden, fitting effortlessly into any scheme, and will grow almost anywhere provided it is in sun.

Trachelospermum jasminoides is a choice climber for the urban space. It is evergreen and laced with luxuriously scented white blooms all summer long.

Reliable plants such as *Acanthus spinosus* can be hard to come by. Striking and architectural, it mixes well with other plants without becoming overpowering.

Eryngium bourgatii 'G .S. Thomas' is a spiky herbaceous perennial that provides fabulous drama when used in large singular groups or contrasted against the texture of grasses.

Trachelospermum jasminoides (zones 8–10) is a sophisticated climber, an evergreen jasmine that has it all: looks, charm and personality. It can be a prima donna, being slightly tender in more exposed areas and taking time to get going, only growing when the plant feels the moment is right. Pander to your plant by providing fertile, well-drained soil in sun and watering and feeding regularly. You will be rewarded with glossy, evergreen leaves, with masses of starry white flowers bursting forth in summer with an amazing perfume that floats through the air from one end of the garden to the other. A relatively slow grower (another plus in the small garden), *T. jasminoides* will reach 3 x 3m (10 x 10ft) in ten years.

Acanthus spinosus (zones 5–9) has deeply cut leaves so handsome that they were often featured on the carved columns of ancient Greece. The flower-spikes, which rise from this mass of divided, spine-tipped foliage, are equally impressive. Appearing from early summer, white blooms with purple bracts reach a majestic 1m (3ft) high spike. *A. spinosus* is generally hardier than the more familiar *A. mollis*, which can be killed off by too much wet. To guarantee the best results, give *A. spinosus* some room. Though herbaceous, a single plant can occupy 1 x 1m (3 x 3ft) without any problems. Grow it in well-drained soil in sun or light shade, with a good layer of mulch through its first winter.

Eryngium bourgatii 'G. S. Thomas' (zones 5–8) has prickly grey-and-white-veined leaves that form a neat tussock of foliage for the centre of the herbaceous border. These striking leaves allow the sea holly to be associated with a good number of plants. *E. bourgatii* forms a good contrast to the smooth large leaves of bergenia, looks good with purple-stained sage or among other heat-loving plants such as lavender, rock roses and santolina, and of course looks great against wafting tufts of grasses. Near translucent violet-blue flowers are produced upon bare blue stems in mid- to late summer to form an unusual display. Due to its sharp, prickly leaves and overall height of up to 50cm (20in), it is perhaps best kept out of arms reach in the family garden.

A free-flowering evergreen favourite, *Hemerocallis* 'Golden Chimes' is reliable, prolific and, above all, exceptionally beautiful.

Free-flowering plants with large heads of true blue flowers, the Headbourne Hybrids are the hardiest form of *Agapanthus*.

The ubiquitous jungle plant, *Chamaerops humilis* is a great plant that will provide drama, structure and a fabulous focal point for your planting schemes.

Hemerocallis 'Golden Chimes' (zones 3–9), also known as the daylily, has star-shaped, deep golden-yellow flowers, streaked with maroon at the backs of their petals. Its stems and buds are an unusual reddish brown. Many consider the daylily to be the perfect perennial plant; the genus comprises thousands of varieties in a rainbow of colours, shapes and sizes. It is extremely tolerant of a wide range of climates, soil types and conditions, is drought-resistant and almost pest- and disease-free. Combine this with a long flowering period and it is easy to see why this plant is so perfect. Though it prefers full sun, this plant will grow in partial shade without loosing any of its colouring. Its eventual height is 90cm (36in).

Agapanthus Headbourne Hybrids (zones 6–11) were developed from the original South African species in the Hon. Lewis Palmer's garden at Headbourne Worthy in Hampshire. As they were bred in the UK, this makes them much hardier than the original form. Plant them in well-drained fertile soil in a sunny, sheltered spot and you will be guaranteed a touch of the exotic without the fear of losing them through the winter. The 50cm (20in) tall flowers bloom for many weeks, and the seed heads are also attractive.

Chamaerops humilis (zones 6–11) originates from the dry scrub and rocky, sandy slopes of the west Mediterranean, and is commonly known as the Mediterranean fan palm. This means that this palm will grow in the poorest of soils, and though it prefers sun, it will tolerate light shade. Once established, this palm is tolerant of the cold, surviving temperatures as low as –10°C (14°F), but until then it will require some winter protection. Wrap it in horticultural fleece or a layer of straw to keep frost at bay during the coldest months. This is a bushy palm, rarely reaching over 2–3m (6–10ft) in height, so it is perfectly suited to the smaller space.

COURTYARD GARDEN

In the tiniest of urban gardens, it is important to resist the urge to cram in as many features or plants as possible. Your enthusiasm, rather than creating an eclectic, interesting look, will result in confusing pandemonium. Instead, keep the garden's design pared down and simple to create one of the most successful urban garden genres: the courtyard garden. Courtyard gardens are often paved to reduce maintenance and are usually enclosed to maximize privacy. Alongside mood and style, practicalities of function (entertaining, sunbathing, planting and storage to name but a few) need to be considered thoroughly for the space to truly be successful. Think calm, not clutter.

PLANNING the GARDEN

Due to his working responsibilities, the owner of this garden was forced to move to the city from a house in the country with a large, mature garden. A keen gardener, he craved the greenery of his old, much loved garden and could not bear the confines of his newly acquired postage-stamp plot.

However, as designer, lack of space was not my only consideration. Though he was keen to potter and garden, enjoying the mechanics, maintenance and care that a garden requires, my client's job would mean that he would be working regularly away from home. Sadly for both of us, his available time to spend on upkeep would be minimal; the garden would be left to its own devices for up to a couple of weeks at a time. I immediately turned my eye to the grassy lawn covering … and raised an eyebrow.

Given the confines of space, time and light, a lawn would be difficult to maintain, and after a long trip away, would the owner really want to tame a jungle of knee-high grass? The lawn was on the 'to go' list.

But we could keep other existing features. Every garden needs storage, and this space included a large shed. Well constructed and built upon a solid base, it would be a genuine waste even to contemplate getting rid of it, and given its large size, it would be problematic to move. However, when viewed directly from the French windows of the living room, the shed was occupying the garden's prime focal point – not exactly the

A colourful mix of plants in the garden's main border is held together with a relaxed sprinkling of grasses and a backdrop of natural willow fencing.

most attractive vista. Luckily for us, it was built in the north-facing section of the garden and therefore occupied an area with the least amount of light, but it was important that the focus was taken away from this view with some kind of screen.

A tree had been planted by the previous owner and was now reasonably mature; a statuesque *Gleditsia triacanthus* 'Sunburst', a beautiful tree and indeed one of my favourites. But we are not all lucky enough to inherit something as elegant and attractive as this. If an ugly mature plant overshadows your garden, think twice before removing it. Your tree could be under the control of a Tree Preservation Order, particularly if you live in a conservation area. If you are unsure, contact your local planning authority and speak to a tree officer. If your tree is protected, you will need written permission to remove it or do any tree surgery.

There was no way that our tree was going anywhere; we were both in awe of it. A definite plus in the garden, this remaining tree would lend a sense of maturity to the whole space, even when it was newly constructed. I would need to design the new garden around it.

Another fortunate inheritance was the neutral, well-cultivated loamy ground and a south-facing aspect (which meant the garden received lots of light), giving this garden a lot of potential even though it was small. My job was just to tap into that potential and exploit it to the full.

COURTYARD GARDEN

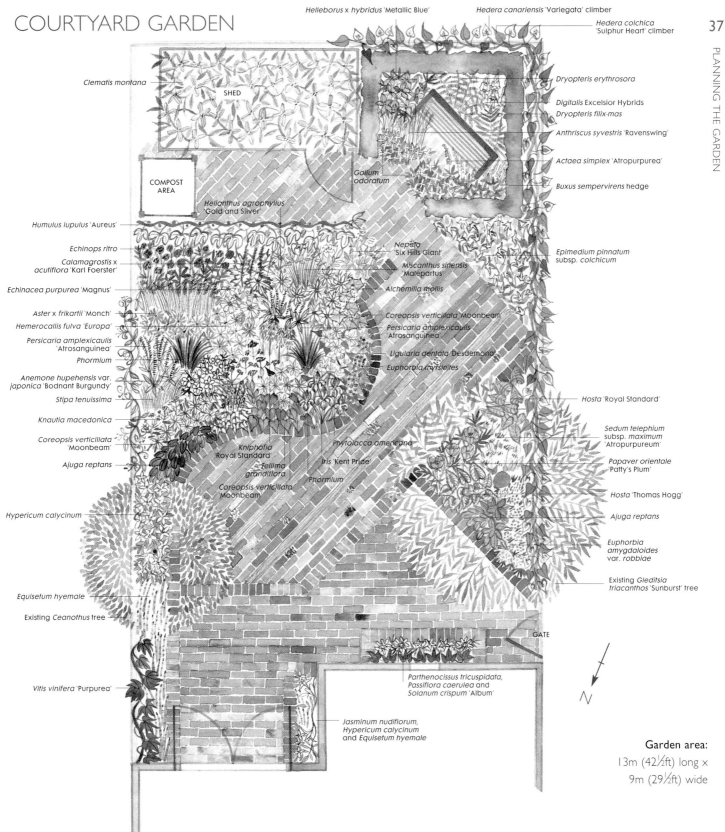

Helleborus x *hybridus* 'Metallic Blue'

Hedera canariensis 'Variegata' climber

Hedera colchica 'Sulphur Heart' climber

Clematis montana

SHED

Dryopteris erythrosora

Digitalis Excelsior Hybrids

Dryopteris filix-mas

Anthriscus syvestris 'Ravenswing'

Actaea simplex 'Atropurpurea'

Buxus sempervirens hedge

COMPOST AREA

Galium odoratum

Helianthus agrophyllus 'Gold and Silver'

Humulus lupulus 'Aureus'

Echinops ritro

Nepeta 'Six Hills Giant'

Epimedium pinnatum subsp. *colchicum*

Calamagrostis x *acutiflora* 'Karl Foerster'

Miscanthus sinensis 'Malepartus'

Echinacea purpurea 'Magnus'

Alchemilla mollis

Aster x *frikartii* 'Monch'

Coreopsis verticillata 'Moonbeam'

Hemerocallis fulva 'Europa'

Persicaria amplexicaulis 'Atrosanguinea'

Persicaria amplexicaulis 'Atrosanguinea'

Ligularia dentata 'Desdemona'

Phormium

Euphorbia myrsinites

Anemone hupehensis var. *japonica* 'Bodnant Burgundy'

Hosta 'Royal Standard'

Stipa tenuissima

Knautia macedonica

Phytolacca americana

Sedum telephium subsp. *maximum* 'Atropurpureum'

Coreopsis verticillata 'Moonbeam'

Kniphofia 'Royal Standard'

Iris 'Kent Pride'

Papaver orientale 'Patty's Plum'

Ajuga reptans

Tellima grandiflora

Phormium

Coreopsis verticillata 'Moonbeam'

Hosta 'Thomas Hogg'

Ajuga reptans

Hypericum calycinum

Euphorbia amygdaloides var. *robbiae*

Existing *Gleditsia triacanthos* 'Sunburst' tree

Equisetum hyemale

Existing *Ceanothus* tree

GATE

Parthenocissus tricuspidata, *Passiflora caerulea* and *Solanum crispum* 'Album'

Vitis vinifera 'Purpurea'

Jasminum nudiflorum, *Hypericum calycinum* and *Equisetum hyemale*

N

Garden area:
13m (42½ft) long x
9m (29½ft) wide

SPECIAL FEATURES

The owner would only have limited time to spend in the garden despite his love of plants, so it was imperative that I made sure the time spent in his space was enhanced by the planting, no matter the time of year. The garden needed to be as alive as possible, creating a constantly changing picture where plants marked the passage of time through seasonal change without ever becoming dull. This was a big challenge, particularly in such a small space. I had to ensure the eye was caught and taken into the space rather than out to the boundaries. The best way to achieve this was to place the visual focus upon a vista of individual ever-changing blooms. Herbaceous perennials were my answer.

That meant there would be an absence of evergreen structure in the winter. Given the maintenance issues, the hard landscaping would therefore have to contribute interest in the winter months. I wanted the paving and screening to look good in itself but also to form a frame for autumn plants, summer seed-heads and spent plant skeletons, so there would be something to look at all year round.

The patio

The garden needed to connect to the large Edwardian house it flowed from to create the outdoor room experience so essential to urban living today.

Due to the garden's diminutive size, I wanted to create the illusion of space. The most effective way to do this was to construct a new terrace using the same materials as those used in the house walls, repeating not only the brick type but also the pattern used when laying the new surface. This would provide the linkage I wanted between house and garden. The small unit size of bricks kept surfacing in proportion to the garden's small size, so adding to the illusion of space.

With materials from the house walls reflected on the garden's floor, the surface area of a garden can be tied to the larger expanse of walls within the house, making a terrace seem bigger than it really is. If you need help identifying and sourcing the brick used in the construction of your house, take a photograph or a sample to a supplier with a brick library, who will be happy to find a suitable match. Not all bricks will be suitable for use as a flooring material, but the supplier will be able to advise on the best substitute.

Selection over, it was time to choose the direction in which to lay the bricks. 'Stretcher bond' pattern matched with the existing brickwork, and to give the garden more width this pattern was laid across the main line of vision from the French windows. Lines laid across the plane of movement in this way subconsciously make the garden user slow down their pace, encouraging them to linger and admire what lies around them.

Left Wooden railway sleepers running among the diagonal brick paving through the main planting area emphasize the longest plane within the garden and make the space seem larger than it really is.

In the small urban garden, wide planting beds like this make it easier to create a succession of seasonal interest.

However, using this pattern throughout the garden would have been overpowering and would not have used the available space to its best advantage. I decided to turn the brick pattern diagonally to maximize the longest axis within the garden. The brick area was further softened with the inclusion of planed timber railway sleepers to create an accent and again emphasize the diagonal length of the garden. They also stopped the garden from looking too traditional. An occasional brick missing here and there to form planting pockets relaxed the whole effect and allowed another opportunity for colour.

The screen

Every garden has those areas you would rather not have in full view, be it the bins, storage tanks or, as here, the garden shed. The obvious answer is to screen the eyesore out. Consider the kind of screening that you use carefully. For example, a diamond or square trellis planted with climbers will take a few seasons to fill out, all the while attracting rather than distracting attention. A more solid barrier, such as the woven willow hurdle used here, is effective from the moment it is erected – absolutely necessary in any small space.

Willow was chosen not only because it provided a visually impenetrable barrier, but also because it complemented the other materials used in the garden so well. Always consider the way in which your choice of features affects other elements within the garden, rather than choosing something because it is appealing at the moment of selection (that is, unless your instincts are usually spot on – garden centres can be dangerous places for the garden shopaholic).

Placed about 1m (3ft) in front of the shed, the willow screening helped to create a small hidden walkway, providing easy access to the shed as well as a small hidden storage area at one end to house a compost bin. This walkway also brought the whole screen closer to the eye, camouflaging the shed much more effectively; indeed, from the house only the roof of the shed remained in view. This problem was solved by planting *Clematis montana* up the side of the shed, then over it to produce a flurry of soft pink flowers in spring and a good disguise throughout the rest of the summer. As well as providing camouflage, the screen was also a perfect backdrop to the main planting bed.

With its emphasis on plants, the garden looks great when viewed from the house. The French windows literally frame the view.

The main planting border

With so much brickwork, it was important to soften the patio area with as much planting as possible. A curving brick edge was used to differentiate the bed from the paving, with its sweeping shape allowing the eye to flow over informal, successional planting.

There is no denying that this is a large planting area for such a small space. Measuring almost 3m (10ft) deep at its widest point, this depth is important in order to include as many plants as possible. Shallow borders negate the possibility of real depth in your planting, making for fewer plants in less space and resulting in little interest. Here, a succession of seasonal change is easier to create. Viewed through the French windows that lead into the garden from the main living space, the border looks very different in spring than in late summer, and in winter there is a plethora of plants held in frosted suspension.

The way to achieve a degree of fullness, maturity and seasonal variation in a large bed is ultimately by overplanting the area. This cramming together of plants does raise a maintenance issue. Plants will require regular splitting and division as they mature once a year in autumn, and though this can be hard work, it totals a lot less maintenance than the almost daily care of containers that many courtyard gardens contain – an impossible task for a much-absent owner.

Lighting was also included through the beds so that alfresco evenings could be enjoyed, and ageing plant silhouettes and seed-heads could be viewed from the comfort of an armchair inside with the onset of winter.

Linked to the main garden by the use of the same brick paving (though used as a loosely paved surface so that plants can grow through it), the far corner of the garden features a low box hedge to suggest separation. A bench invites the user to sit and enjoy the view.

PLANTS and PLANTING

As the owner was a keen gardener, I wanted the space to be a tranquil, leafy paradise that would take him away from the noisy bustle of the street just outside the front door and far from the stresses and pressures of working life.

A mature tree immediately adds height to a garden but a mature umbrella of foliage also casts shadows and light shade. After removing the lower branches of the *Gleditsia tracanthos* 'Sunburst' to lift the crown, this area became the perfect place to sit and enjoy relaxing Sunday mornings and sociable Saturday nights. I was also lucky enough to inherit many mature climbers into my planting scheme. These blurred the existing boundaries, allowing me to concentrate my efforts on two main planting borders: the large sunny bed that takes centre stage and the very different cool woodland area at the shady rear of the space.

The fresh emerald green leaves of *Galium odoratum*, sprinkled with flower, let you know that spring is well underway and summer will soon be here.

Humulus lupulus 'Aureus' is a great plant for a new garden, quickly covering fences and walls in a season to give that comfortably mature, lived-in look.

Galium odoratum (zones 4–8), a native British plant also known as sweet woodruff, is a helpfully evergreen herbaceous perennial. Spreading by creeping underground rhizomes, it quickly colonizes areas to form the ultimate in low-growing – 25cm (10in) – groundcover. Weave *G. odoratum* through strong-growing herbaceous perennials that will flower after its blooms of have faded, or at the base of shrubs that are yet to grow leaves to form a marvellous spring frame of lush green. In spring through to early summer, heads of blooms dance above the foliage; the flowers are tiny in size but their bright white colour and sheer numbers make them unbelievably striking. *G. odoratum* grows in any soil that is not too acid and thrives in shade. It is an indispensable plant for shady areas.

Humulus lupulus 'Aureus' (zones 3–8) has large leaves, bright attractive foliage, greeny yellow fruits and speedy growth that all make the golden hop immensely desirable. When given support, this twining climber can easily twine its way 6m (20ft) skyward in just one season. Its large architectural foliage of fresh lime green perfectly frames any plants that are set before it. You can also grow it up a large tripod in the centre of a border. Perhaps its only drawback in the garden is its deciduous nature; each year in autumn, spent top growth needs to be removed to within 23cm (9in) of ground level (to provide winter protection) and the remainder pruned to ground level the following spring. However, this arduous task is worthwhile when dealing with such an enthusiastic plant.

All plants have character, but *Equisetum hyemale* is plain bizarre. Add a real talking point to your garden by planting it where it will be noticed.

Do not be deceived by the fragile looking blooms of *Iris germanica* 'Kent Pride'. It is a tough plant that will reward you well with a minimum of maintenance.

If you are unafraid of the heights *Parthenocissus tricuspidata* can scale, it will reward you with quick cover and magnificent autumn colour.

Equisetum hyemale (zones 3–11) produces bizarre leafless stems that rise snakelike from the ground, reaching a height of 45cm (18in) to great dramatic effect. *E. hyemale* is a member of an ancient family of plants dating back millions of years. A British native, growing in water and moist soils, this plant is related to the pernicious weed horsetail, and while it is not nearly so invasive, it still needs to be watched carefully if it is not to run out of control. Although it enjoys damp ground, it will grow in pots if you are not willing to risk letting it loose in your borders. Its common name, scouring rush, refers to the fact that the surface of the plant, like that of all horsetails, has silica crystals embedded in it and was used for cleaning pots and pans before pan scourers.

Iris germanica **'Kent Pride'** (zones 3–10) produces reddy chestnut-brown blooms in early summer; each tall bearded bloom is like a delicate butterfly. *I.g.* 'Kent Pride' is a rhizomatous iris, meaning that it has surface rhizomes that should be partially exposed from the soil where they can receive a good baking from the sun. It is from these rhizomes that the sword-like leaves followed by blooms spring, so treat them with care, particularly when digging through borders. They grow best in groups of three, 15–30cm (6–12in) apart, without mulch (which could cause rotting) and without shade being cast over them from other plants. Lift, divide and replant the rhizomes every 3 to 5 years once their display starts to wane.

Parthenocissus tricuspidata (zones 4–8), also known as Boston ivy, can be a fabulous plant or a pariah, depending upon how you choose to use it. The most important consideration is the area you allow it to cover. Do not underestimate how voraciously this plant will grow. I have seen it covering whole houses if left unchecked. However, if you have the space, Boston ivy is most accommodating. It will grow in any soil that has just enough moisture within it to sustain its structure, is self-clinging (it grows its own pads) and therefore requires no support and will grow well in sun, shade and very inhospitable positions. Take the plunge and you will be rewarded with large, three-lobed green leaves, colouring up to molten crimson and scarlet in autumn.

Helianthus agrophyllus 'Gold and Silver' is an unusual multi-branching annual with unique silver foliage. It also produces plentiful yellow flowers.

Due to its long flowering season and self-supporting lavender-blue daisy flowers, *Aster* x *frikartii* 'Monch' is a much celebrated late summer perennial.

Commonly known as the roadside daylily, *Hemerocallis fulva* 'Europa' is robust and energetic, and given time will bulk up quickly to form large clumps of vibrant orange blooms.

Helianthus agrophyllus 'Gold and Silver' (zones 4–8) is an annual that hails from Texas. Fully hardy, seeds can be sown directly into the ground where they are to flower in spring. Sow the plants thinly, roughly 30cm (12in) apart, into dug-over, cultivated ground that has been raked to a fine tilth, then regularly water your seeds. Once mature, it is the foliage that sets this plant apart from other sunflowers; its large, silver leaves are highly ornamental. Slightly toothed, the leaves (and stems) are covered in silky hairs that are soft to the touch. Multi-branching, each plant holds several bright yellow blooms, each roughly 10cm (4in) across. Its ultimate height is 2m (6ft).

Aster x *frikartii* **'Monch'** (zones 5–10) looks good in any setting, but is particularly attractive when set among the oaty, bleached colours of grasses in a natural 'meadow' scheme. Like so many plants, it enjoys well-drained, open soil in full sun and, given these conditions, will flower for a good three to four months from midsummer. Do beware if you stray from these planting ideals – on heavy soils, for example, you may lose your plants in a cold wet winter. The ultimate height of this fine perennial is 70cm (28in), with a spread of 40cm (16in).

Hemerocallis fulva 'Europa' (zones 3–9) is one of the first varieties of daylily to burst into bloom, its bright orange flowers positively fizzing with colour. These cheerful flowers, as with all daylilies, only last a day but successively flower for weeks. It is not commonly known that daylilies have been used in Chinese cooking for centuries. Both the buds and petals can be eaten; they are crunchy, tasty and peppery. With such a plethora of flower, you will not miss a few. The flowerbuds look great chopped up in a salad. Provide your daylilies with fertile, moist, well-drained soil, dividing your plants every three years or so to maintain their vigour. *H. f.* 'Europa' will reach an overall height and spread of 1 x 1.2m (3 x 4ft).

Miscanthus sinensis 'Malepartus' forms an imposing statement with its dense mounds of arching foliage. These long blades produce tall, loose panicles of flowers in midsummer before many other grasses.

With its soft, hairy stems catching in the wind, and its flowers and foliage fluffed like the bristles on a traditional shaving brush, *Stipa tenuissima* adds elegance and grace to the garden.

The clashing contrast between the magenta horizontal petals and the central disc of deep orange makes *Echinacea purpurea* 'Magnus' difficult to ignore.

Miscanthus sinensis **'Malepartus'** (zones 5–9) begins to flower in midsummer, its rich reddish plum panicles reaching over 2m (6ft) in height. With time, these tight panicles fluff out to form feathery plumes of white, which turn to silvery buff as they become parched by the sun's rays. Unless hit by strong winds, these flower-heads will remain upon the plant through the winter, adding much to the winter garden when laced with a scattering of frost. Autumn sees the foliage colour up, the blades achieving autumnal tones of red, gold and orange. Though this grass is tolerant of most conditions, it performs best in moist, fertile, well-drained soil in sun. The overall height of the foliage is 1.5m (5ft), with a spread of 1.2m (4ft).

Stipa tenuissima (zones 7–11) adds much to the garden's profile from spring onwards. This is when its loose, airy panicles first open, remaining until they submit to the first frosts of autumn. It flowers continually throughout this period, making it one of the most free flowering of all the grasses. The flower-heads catch in the slightest of breezes, so it is one of few plants that can effectively contribute movement to the garden scene. Unlike so many plants, *S. tenuissima* prefers poor soil in which to grow, too many nutrients making it flop in the centre, but it does need sun to perform well. Plant it within borders, beside informal paths, in planting pockets within informal terraces or in the gravel garden. It will reach an overall height of 60cm (24in).

Echinacea purpurea **'Magnus'** (zones 3–8) is an architecturally striking plant originating from the dry prairies of North and Central America. Stiff flower-heads are borne from midsummer until early autumn to give a fine display at the end of the season. Unfortunately this plant dislikes competition from other plants, so you may find that you lose it from your borders after only a couple of years. However, its structural magnificence and bold colour make the plant well worthy of replacement. Grow *E. p.* 'Magnus' in deep, well-drained, humus-rich soil in full sun, though it will tolerate some shade. Cutting back faded blooms will often lead to a second flush of flower. Its ultimate height is 90cm (3ft).

SMALL TOWN GARDEN

A tight budget plus a small space does not have to result in a dull garden. By keeping things simple but visually strong, you will create a space that cannot help but work. Here, a sheet of timber decking extended to traverse a wide band of water is the key highlight of the garden. It links one area to another and seemingly floats above and at the heart of a sea of planting. Anchored by a row of upright bamboo poles to form an upward thrust, the eye is brought all the way through the space, resting on different areas of interest along the way.

My clients wanted to reclaim some of their outdoor space from their growing children to form an area for themselves in which to relax, eat and entertain, with a little bit of wow factor thrown in for good measure. They did not want it to be too modern – with any investment of hard-earned cash, it is important your garden does not quickly date.

Like so many working couples, though interested in gardening, they could not afford the time their hobby demanded, but knew that they both had a love of plants. Seasonal interest, fragrance and lots to look at were key requirements of the planting plan.

PLANNING the GARDEN

The clients wanted the garden to link to the house to provide as seamless a transition as possible. There were lots of entrances and exits into this small space that all required new vistas: French windows leading from the drawing room straight out into the garden were of great importance; there was access from the side of the property and also from the rear corner; and a door led directly from the garden space into the garage. In a small garden, this was a lot to accommodate, so time was taken to consider how to keep all this available and yet not too obvious, and to ensure that the views would be interesting all year round.

The clients' practical requirements were simple: to screen the garage, get rid of the high-maintenance grass and replace it with an area that made the most of the evening sun for entertaining, relaxing and generally admiring the view. Even in this average-sized garden, they wanted separate areas for different functions, so the garden needed to work together as a whole while still evoking different moods as one journeyed through the space.

One of the owners was a keen gardener, so I was lucky enough to have a site where the soil had been conditioned well over the years. It was a rich, moisture-retentive loam, so only a minimum of soil conditioner was required and an application of fish, blood and bone, a slow-release fertilizer, just to give new plants as good a start as possible.

With the focus on entertaining, it was important that a new seating area was incorporated where it would receive the last rays of the evening sun. The garden was east facing, so towards the back of the garden seemed the obvious choice. However, this would be in front of a domineering brick-built garage, so we would need to soften and possibly screen this backdrop to integrate it into the space rather than let it take over.

A sense of journey was very important. Even in the smallest of gardens, a feeling of space can be created by adding lots of distinct areas with pathways leading you to and from them. The existing straight path had very little interest to it, simply leading the user from one end of the garden to the other. By using diagonals and the garden's width, the garden could be made to seem far larger than it actually was.

The high-maintenance grass was soon to be history, to be replaced with gravel and plantings within it to break up any large expanses. I also wanted to create a new dimension to the garden by introducing a large expanse of water across its width. This would not only create a new planting arena for the owners to enjoy, but would also reflect the sky, create a feeling of gentle, quiet relaxation that only water provides and, with a bridge over it, add to the sense of journey and adventure.

To create a strong, cohesive scheme, choose plants that work with rather than against your hard landscaping.

SMALL TOWN GARDEN

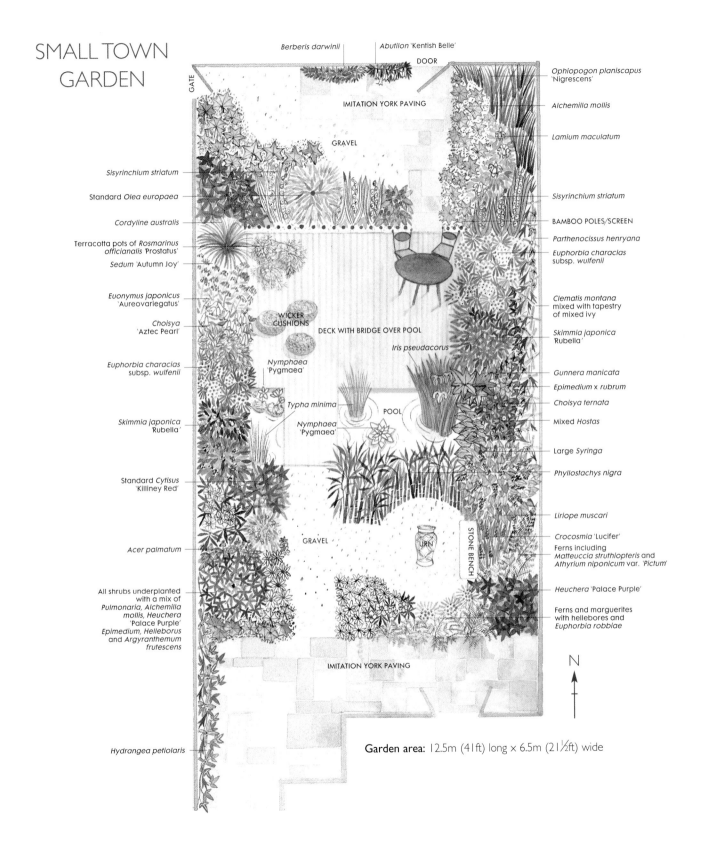

GATE

Berberis darwinii

Abutilon 'Kentish Belle'

DOOR

IMITATION YORK PAVING

GRAVEL

Ophiopogon planiscapus 'Nigrescens'

Alchemilla mollis

Lamium maculatum

Sisyrinchium striatum

Standard *Olea europaea*

Cordyline australis

Terracotta pots of *Rosmarinus officianalis* 'Prostatus'

Sedum 'Autumn Joy'

Euonymus japonicus 'Aureovariegatus'

Choisya 'Aztec Pearl'

Euphorbia characias subsp. *wulfenii*

Skimmia japonica 'Rubella'

Standard *Cytisus* 'Killiney Red'

Acer palmatum

All shrubs underplanted with a mix of *Pulmonaria, Alchemilla mollis, Heuchera* 'Palace Purple' *Epimedium, Helleborus* and *Argyranthemum frutescens*

Hydrangea petiolaris

Sisyrinchium striatum

BAMBOO POLES/SCREEN

Parthenocissus henryana

Euphorbia characias subsp. *wulfenii*

Clematis montana mixed with tapestry of mixed ivy

Skimmia japonica 'Rubella'

Gunnera manicata

Epimedium x *rubrum*

Choisya ternata

Mixed *Hostas*

Large *Syringa*

Phyllostachys nigra

Liriope muscari

Crocosmia 'Lucifer'

Ferns including *Matteuccia struthiopteris* and *Athyrium niponicum* var. 'Pictum'

Heuchera 'Palace Purple'

Ferns and marguerites with hellebores and *Euphorbia robbiae*

WICKER CUSHIONS

DECK WITH BRIDGE OVER POOL

Nymphaea 'Pygmaea'

Iris pseudacorus

Typha minima

Nymphaea 'Pygmaea'

POOL

GRAVEL

URN

STONE BENCH

IMITATION YORK PAVING

N

Garden area: 12.5m (41ft) long × 6.5m (21½ft) wide

SPECIAL FEATURES

It was of paramount importance to me that the special features within the space would appear visually soft so that the garden wrapped the house without dominating it. There was to be no hard-edged paving or stainless steel here; natural materials such as timber, bamboo, water and gravel give an understated, unpretentious look – perfect for relaxation.

Surfacing

Though many of us like the look (and indeed the feel underfoot) of a swathe of green lawn in a garden, grass requires an investment of time in order to keep it looking its best. When you are working full time, the commitment of a cut once or twice a week, feeding, scarifying and so on can become a painful, time-consuming chore. Gravel is a cheap, attractive option, and though essentially a hard landscape material, it is made up of tiny pieces of shingle and therefore remains soft and easy on the eye. You can lay it directly on the ground (or on top of a layer of hardcore in larger, heavily trafficked spaces), but in essence you will simply be creating an extra large area of mulch for your plantings. I find that this can quickly become colonized by weeds rather than those choice plants you want to encourage to self-seed. You should therefore always use a weedproof membrane (it comes off the roll in sheet form from all large garden centres) and cut slits into it in order to plant through it. In time, a layer of soil will build up naturally on top of this membrane and plants will find their way naturally. Do not apply too thick a layer of gravel or walking on it will feel awkward and spongy, as if you have landed on the moon.

In this garden, a second gravel area was created to the rear of the decking. Repeating materials in this way helps give the garden a coordinated character.

A stone seat, within its own circle of gravel and natural planting, creates a tranquil space for quiet contemplation.

Decking and bridge

I always feel that decks and planes of water go hand in hand, and with such a large expanse of water, decking seemed the obvious choice. Although I love hardwood decking materials, a tanalized, treated softwood was used here to keep within budget. With a ribbed finish, this would keep the area non-slip, which is important next to water with energetic young teenagers running around.

Below & right The wooden deck hosts formal iron seating. The linear design of the metalwork is complemented by the natural bamboo screening and the bamboo plants by the pond.

Always pay attention to the direction in which your decking is laid. Because the water feature utilized the width of the space here, I chose to lay planks running lengthways to the garden. This not only created a tension within the space, but easily allowed a section of boards to extend into a bridge, inviting one across the water and on to the seating area itself. The bridge was purposely created to be wide enough to ensure that two people could walk side-by-side at a leisurely pace.

Formal and informal seating options accommodate different requirements and ages of user beside a timber-edged pool.

Pool

Water features within the small garden are a positive experience, creating babbling sound, reflections, movement and light as well as encouraging wildlife. So often in a small garden we feel that we have to use as small a feature as possible, but this can be a mistake. If you want a pool, why not go for it and make a real statement. Traversing almost the entire width of the garden, this formal, timber-edged pool is certainly that. In a garden where every scrap of space has to count, formal shapes work better than organic wildlife pools that can become a touch contrived. Here, a rectangular expanse of water runs slightly beneath the deck to create the illusion that the deck itself is floating on water. A planting shelf allows for marginal planting, while a deep central expanse allows for miniature water lilies, fish and lots of oxygenating plants, which ensures that the water does not become a stagnant home for mosquitoes.

Screen

If you have a small space, a transparent screen suggests partition and provides a visual full stop without light and space being sacrificed. I used thick bamboo poles sunk into the ground at regular intervals and screwed to the back of the deck for extra strength. The canes were cut at different heights to provide visual interest and were loosely spaced so that the planting behind them could be admired anywhere in the garden. This casual screening behind the decking area took the onus off the bricked garage at the rear of the garden, and forced the eye through the garden and up into the air, forming a fantastic vertical accent so often lacking in small gardens.

Seating

A stone seat that had been in the family for some time was separated from the modern seating area and placed within its own circle of gravel and informal, natural planting. With ferns at its back and a semi-screening of loosely scattered bamboo, it became a tranquil green space that would invite the user into quiet relaxation or contemplation.

For more relaxed afternoon loafing, a set of three woven cushions were perfect for lounging and lazing around. Behind them, three containers of prostrate rosemary echoed the circular shapes of the three cushions as well as enhancing the garden with flower and scent.

The circular shapes of these woven cushions and pots of prostrate rosemary create a pleasing arrangement against the bamboo screen.

PLANTS and PLANTINGS

To achieve a real sense of passing seasons, it was important to use plants from all walks of life: evergreen shrubs mixed with deciduous climbers that would flower at different times of year, herbaceous perennials to provide accents of bloom, groundcover to ensure a carpet of foliage or flower throughout the year, bulbs and, of course, water plants for the pond.

Many genres of planting to include, I know, but with the lawn gone, the area available for planting was fairly large. I used lots of Mediterranean plants that always look good in gravel. This included an olive among a carpet of evergreen *Sisyrinchium striatum* 'Aunt May', and margeurites jostling with euphorbias and lavender.

The pond allowed for a verdant *Gunnera manicata* destined to grow huge and play with the sense of scale of the space. Water plants such as *Iris pseudacorus*, *Typha minima* and *Juncus effusus* were planted in baskets to contain their eventual size, while a scattering of bamboo separated the gravel area from the deck and pool; these would provide a living screen echoing the upright poles and also offer sound and movement.

As a designer I was lucky that the owners had encouraged a tapestry of green climbers to clothe the fences, so the garden's boundaries were less obvious. A mature *Clematis montana*, ivy and honeysuckle smothered the right fence; euonymous and *Hydrangea petiolaris* did their best on the left.

Argyranthemum frutescens is the perfect accompaniment to gravel, creating a picture of understated simplicity.

With the protection of a south-facing sheltered wall, why not try out the exotic blooms of *Abutilon* 'Kentish Belle'?

Argyranthemum frutescens (zones 9–11) is the plant for you if you hanker for daisies. Hailing from the Canary Islands, we tend to treat these sub-shrubs as annuals, though in a sheltered southern garden you may find that marguerites make it through the winter. If you forget to lift yours in autumn but notice new life creeping through the soil the following spring, simply cut back any dead growth and pinch out the growing tips to ensure a bushy plant. The best form of insurance if you do not want to take this risk is to take cuttings in autumn from non-flowering shoots; these are easy to propagate in a greenhouse or on a windowsill, as most varieties do not come true from seed. Plant new plants in spring into well-drained soil in full sun and they will bloom all summer, even if your deadheading is somewhat erratic. Marguerites are at home with perennials and grasses, are stunning in containers and are often trained into lollipop standards.

Abutilon 'Kentish Belle' (zones 8–10) can be grown directly in free-draining soil in milder areas, with a protective wall. Remember that a combination of cold and wet is the surest way to kill your new wall shrub. The foliage may die back in winter, but normally renews from ground level in spring. With its large graceful yellow flowers, each with a red calyx hanging below and handsome foliage, 'Kentish Belle' is a prolific flowerer and you will be surprised at how vigorously it will grow when free from the confines of a pot. However, in colder areas the safer option is to grow it as a containerized specimen, moving it into a greenhouse or conservatory when temperatures begin to plummet. This plant is easy to grow from cuttings taken in spring and summer.

If you have a large expanse of wall in shade, brighten it up with the self-clinging wall shrub *Hydrangea petiolaris*.

Swords of evergreen leaves of *Sisyrinchium striatum* 'Aunt May' strike up from the ground to form an eye-catching dramatic perennial.

Epimedium x *rubrum* will develop slowly in dry shade but will cover ground more quickly in rich, damp leaf mould.

Hydrangea petiolaris (zones 4–8) may be slow to establish but will grow to great heights, clinging on with small aerial roots and growing to 15m (49ft) if unchecked. Make sure that you do not get more than you bargained for, though unruly stems can be cut back in autumn to quell its exuberance. Its attractive lace-cap flowers will reliably brighten up a shady side passage to your property, flowering in early summer to cover the plant completely. Though deciduous, mahogany brown stems with peeling bark can be most attractive in winter. *H. petiolaris* is perfectly well mannered as far as soil requirement is concerned, flourishing on both alkaline and acid soils; just make sure you keep it well watered when young to promote its establishment.

Sisyrinchium striatum 'Aunt May' (zones 4–8) has iris-like leaves, each boldly striped with creamy yellow to punch through other plantings or confidently stand alone in drifts. The evergreen foliage means this plant can hold its own in the border at any time of year, not only when flowering in early to midsummer. Creamy yellow flowers are held above the foliage for many weeks. Do not be too quick with the secateurs; often a stem that looks over will suddenly produce more blooms. This plant loves hot, balmy conditions and will clump up given time to form drought-tolerant groups, fantastic in gravel or among cobbles or boulders. It is one of those 'must-have' plants that is easy to grow even for the complete novice.

Epimedium x *rubrum* (zones 4–8) hugs the ground like the scales on a fish. Though on the whole evergreen, old leaves are best cut back in spring just as the new leaves emerge to reveal the tiny but beautiful delicate flowers secreted within a ground canopy of lovely foliage. Species of *Epimedium* are sometimes tinged bronze in spring and almost all colour up well in the autumn to form a carpet of invaluable colour throughout the year. Amazingly dainty, *E.* x *rubrum* flowers rose red with russet autumn leaf colour, *E. grandiflorum* 'White Queen' produces large white flowers, while 'Lilafee' bears masses of rosy-lilac blooms. To ensure impact, plant them at roughly six plants per square metre (yard), and provide them with a deep winter mulch each year to promote health and vigour.

There is no denying that for many people hostas have irresistible appeal, and attractive *Hosta undulata* var. *univittata* is simply the tip of the iceberg.

Shade beneath trees is an almost impossible situation for plants to grow but *Euphorbia amygdaloides* var. *robbiae* impressively rises to this challenge.

Jasminum officinale is a pretty, vigorous climber, suitable for covering large areas and with the added bonus of marvellous scent.

Hosta undulata **var.** *univittata* (zones 3–8) is a centrally marked, medium-sized hosta. Its glossy mass of gently arching leaves with bold white stripes adds elegant interest to cool shade. Reaching 45 x 70cm (18 x 28in) when mature, early to mid-summer sees the addition of attractive mauve flowers reaching upwards from the foliage. Unfortunately. it is not just gardeners who find hostas attractive; slugs and snails find them extremely tasty, which can lead to unbelievable damage in the blink of an eye. Try to control these pests by using organic slug bait that is not harmful to birds and other wildlife, by growing them in pots capped with a mulch of gravel or by using biological controls.

Euphorbia amygdaloides **var.** *robbiae* (zones 6–9) is a short-lived evergreen perennial, but once planted you never seem to lose it. It spreads rapidly by rhizomes underground, with the parent creating a host of offspring to replace the parent plant. Indeed, the dark green rosettes of foliage, giving rise to a mass of yellow-green spring flowers, can become invasive and will need to be kept in check in the smaller garden; it is even more prolific when allowed the luxury of well-drained fertile soil. However, its valuable nature usually gains it access to the garden. It makes great ground cover in difficult spots, reaching an overall height of roughly 60cm (24in) and a spread that is dependent upon its growing position.

Jasminum officinale (zones 7–10) spreads in all directions to form a dense mass of foliage, each leaf composed in fact of five, seven or nine leaflets in mid- to grey-green. Indeed, if this plant becomes a little too prolific, prune it back hard in late winter or early spring, as it will soon produce new growth on which blooms will be produced that same year. Although this plant will grow on any soil type and in almost any aspect (except very exposed spots), a moist soil or regular watering will encourage the most growth. Allow the jasmine plenty of room in order fully to appreciate the mass of heavenly scented white flowers produced from midsummer through early autumn. Its ultimate height and spread is 10 x 10m (33 x 33ft).

Slower growing than its rather more enthusiastic cousins, *Parthenocissus henryana* is more demure and infinitely more elegant, providing an attractive foliage display in both summer and autumn.

Grown in moist, rich soil, *Pulmonaria saccharata* makes a valuable contribution to the spring woodland border with its delicate flowers and attractive leaves.

Sword-like leaves sprinkled with a plethora of vibrant scarlet blooms makes the clump-forming *Crocosmia* 'Lucifer' an easy and popular plant.

Parthenocissus henryana (zones 6–9), or Chinese Virginia creeper, has foliage where three or five leaflets group to form stars of green, each marked with beautiful silver-white veining. The foliage deepens to a purple-red throughout the summer, finally pulling out all the stops to provide an autumnal high of vivid orange and fiery scarlet. Growing well on very acid soil or soil with high alkalinity, *P. henryana* prefers the cover of some shade, as full sun will weaken the pretty silvery veining. Although this plant does produce tendrils on which to support itself, the plants grow heavy with age and it is wise to provide a framework of wires to support it at maturity. Ten years will see this woody climber cover an area of 3 x 3m (10 x 10ft) but full maturity can see it reach twice this height and spread.

Pulmonaria saccharata (zones 3–8), or lungwort, is valued for its felty-green, polka-dot leaves that may persist through a mild winter (cut the old foliage back before the end of winter to make way for new). It should be divided every few years in order to propagate the true parent plant as, though readily produced, self-seeded plants do not come true from seed, leading to some interesting variations. Also, be aware that *P. saccharata* can be susceptible to powdery mildew through dry conditions, so keep your plants well watered and keep an eye out for slug and snail damage. Tiny flowers are produced in spring above the foliage in shades of violet, red-violet and white. The plant reaches a mature height and spread of 30 x 60cm (12 x 24in).

Crocosmia 'Lucifer' (zones 5–9) is a fantastically easy-to-grow perennial (plants grow from corms), preferring fertile, moist, well-drained soil in sun or partial shade. It is very quick growing and can become invasive if left to its own devices for too long, so don't let it get out of control. Branched, arching spikes of flame-red bloom are produced in mid- to late summer, forming a splash of colour that associates brilliantly with grasses. Use it to fill up awkward spaces in your borders or at your patio's edge, where it will create an eye-catching display up to 1–1.2m (3–4ft) in height.

BOARDWALK GARDEN

This garden is the ultimate laidback space in which to work, rest and play. An aged brick wall enveloping the garden provides the perfect backdrop to the small divided areas, each separate yet split with the minimum of division so you will never feel isolated. A snake of lawn, a waist-height veil of grasses mixed with bright perennials, decking, a swathe of turf and a smattering of brick surfacing all mingle together with no single area dominating another.

The materials here are natural, handmade or reclaimed, which lends the garden the relaxed look of easy living that the owners were so keen to achieve. As their first garden, nothing is too orderly or contrived, so that they can make mistakes without huge holes appearing in the planting. The plants are jungle-inspired at the far end, developing into an unstructured meadow in the middle where the plants themselves can fight it out, with the owners stepping in if one variety gets a little too assertive.

PLANNING the GARDEN

The brief for this garden was very close to my heart. As keen travellers, the owners wanted a garden that would appeal to their sense of adventure and remind them of their brief journeys to far-flung places around the world. They wanted to include as many sensory experiences as possible, so colour, smell and touch were paramount; taste would come from al fresco meals. Though small, the garden would also need to be large enough to accommodate numbers of visitors for those summer barbecues.

Creating an eclectic space is something that I really enjoy – the chance to form separate areas that glide or even collide into one another, while being careful that the whole does not become confusing and disjointed. Plants were to be the linking factor, softening the different areas of hard landscaping and a jungle theme that thins out into an area of informal meadow. Repetition planting would be used to create strong ties within the whole. To unify the space even more, we were lucky enough to have the aged brick wall to surround the area.

The clients also wanted the garden to be environmentally sound, using reclaimed materials where possible and plants that attracted wildlife. The space was to be very green – a kind of wildlife hotel within the corridor of bleak backyards of the big city.

This suggested the inclusion of turf, which, after being out of favour with many designers for so long, seems to be making something of a comeback. The owners were fully prepared for the maintenance required to keep the lawn looking good, a job made more difficult within the confines of a small space. It would require regular cutting, aerating, feeding and scarifying, but they felt this was worthwhile.

The small urban garden allows the luxury of enjoying each and every flower in its own right. In a larger space, an excess of plants may mean individual beauty is overlooked.

I have to agree. In the small garden, provided the lawn area is in proportion to the space itself and that it is not so small as to prove fiddly or so large as to become arduous, a green swathe of grass glows like an emerald. Lawns feel fabulous underfoot, smell great when the grass has just been cut and sparkle after a quick hose down on a summer's evening – all important sensory considerations.

Aspect is important in the garden, not only in governing which plants can be used where, but also in assessing the sunniest situations in the garden at any given time of day. The area that receives the most evening sun is paramount to most city dwellers because this is the place where they will want to sit when they get back after a hard day's slog at work. This garden was west facing, not a bad aspect at all. The rear of the house received sun for much of the day, but the garden's right side would receive the most evening rays. A secondary seating area was definitely required here, preferably becoming a place where scent would also preside.

The soil type was good loam, allowing the maximum amount of plants to be grown, and we were lucky also to have a neutral pH.

However, the garden was not free of problems. Physical problems that would have to be overcome were that the garden was extremely overlooked, particularly to the rear, and that at least a third of the garden was covered with a rather thick slab of concrete. With the only access leading through the house, digging this up and removing it was going to create a huge problem (and potentially a large expense), but one that had to be resolved. Using it as a base for a new deck turned out to be the ideal solution.

BOARDWALK GARDEN

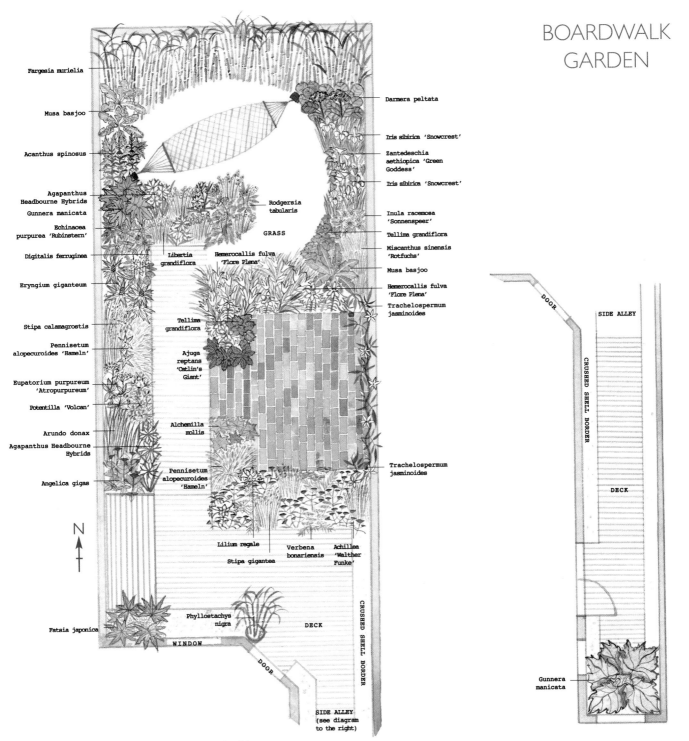

Fargesia murielia

Musa basjoo

Acanthus spinosus

Agapanthus Headbourne Hybrids

Gunnera manicata

Echinacea purpurea 'Rubinstern'

Digitalis ferruginea

Eryngium giganteum

Stipa calamagrostis

Pennisetum alopecuroides 'Hameln'

Eupatorium purpureum 'Atropurpureum'

Potentilla 'Volcan'

Arundo donax

Agapanthus Headbourne Hybrids

Angelica gigas

Libertia grandiflora

Rodgersia tabularis

GRASS

Hemerocallis fulva 'Flore Plena'

Tellima grandiflora

Ajuga reptans 'Catlin's Giant'

Alchemilla mollis

Pennisetum alopecuroides 'Hameln'

Darmera peltata

Iris sibirica 'Snowcrest'

Zantedeschia aethiopica 'Green Goddess'

Iris sibirica 'Snowcrest'

Inula racemosa 'Sonnenspeer'

Tellima grandiflora

Miscanthus sinensis 'Rotfuchs'

Musa basjoo

Hemerocallis fulva 'Flore Plena'

Trachelospermum jasminoides

Trachelospermum jasminoides

Lilium regale

Stipa gigantea

Verbena bonariensis

Achillea 'Walther Funke'

N

Fatsia japonica

Phyllostachys nigra

DECK

WINDOW

DOOR

CRUSHED SHELL BORDER

SIDE ALLEY (see diagram to the right)

DOOR

SIDE ALLEY

CRUSHED SHELL BORDER

DECK

Gunnera manicata

Garden area: 15.5m (51ft) long × 7m (23ft) wide

SPECIAL FEATURES

The features of this garden were to look funky, urban, reclaimed and young. The garden was to have a personality, be fun and be relaxing at the same time. This garden was going to be a place where you could chill out alone or enjoy the sublime, halcyon evenings that only come when sharing your first garden with friends.

The luxury of a brick wall was admittedly an advantage, yet it could easily have become a weighty accent upon the scheme, limiting the garden by enclosure and forcing it to become the traditional cottage garden space that we wanted to avoid.

Deck and boardwalk

The existing concrete patio would provide the site for a deck, helpfully converting into a solid base for the framework that would support the surface boards. A deck would also remove the expense and toil of digging up an expansive area of thick concrete, then carting it away through the house. However, rather than installing a polished deck with fluted boards, this garden required a less sophisticated raw look. I wanted it to be reminiscent of decks found abroad, running through the margins of rainforests, through mountains or across the beaches of Thailand. It needed to look unrefined and functional, as if it had been provided to serve as a simple surface, and to last.

The chosen timber was tanalized to protect it from rotting, and sawn rather than planed to provide a degree of slip resistance. This sawn look also allows the wood to wear down

Right Internal division creates different areas to fulfil several purposes and suit different moods.

Below Living veils of planting formed by tall-growing plants and grasses suggest privacy while losing nothing in spatial terms.

naturally with time, developing its own patina and texture with use (note that this finish is not suitable if you have children because the timber could potentially splinter). It will also colour with age, finding its own character and adding to the garden's personality. To produce a chunky unsophisticated look, each board was generously proportioned at 20 × 5cm (8 × 2in), wider and thicker than manufactured decking boards. Steps here and there added to the sense of journey, making the garden more interesting by creating movement and also providing impromptu seating areas.

The boardwalk acted as an extension to the main decking, extending the seating area into the garden and inviting the user into the space to explore. It skates through two areas of planting, leading directly through the middle of a miniature meadow, where plants provide the scent, colour and texture that is reminiscent of many public boardwalks abroad.

Brick terrace

The secondary seating area would be a terrace that was to be situated in the warmest part of the garden and would butt right up against a brick wall to maximize the size. Where two materials are

Painting your garden's walls white or cream will bounce light back into the tiniest space.

seen at such close quarters, it is imperative that they match exactly or contrast strongly, otherwise the area can look wishy-washy and unconsidered. Here, new London stock bricks will, in time, develop the rich texture of the walls. They were laid in the same stretcher bond pattern as the walls, with the right-angled effect giving the impression that the wall spills out, flowing on to the garden floor.

Unlike reconstituted concrete slabs or stone, all handmade bricks generate a feeling of softness and warmth, and are extremely tactile and pleasant underfoot. However, not all bricks are suitable for use as a surface material outdoors, so check with your supplier before purchasing them as frost damages some bricks, causing them to shatter or 'blow'. This in itself can look extremely attractive in certain situations but it may not be the look that you are aiming to create.

The small modular size of the bricks used in this garden also created the illusion of space; more bricks were used than would have been the case with paving slabs, and the increased jointing helped to give the impression that the terrace occupies a much larger area than it actually does. This is always a good idea in the small garden where every bit of space needs to be made to count.

Deckside, an unusual mulch of crushed shell creates a funky recycled look, and a great visual pun.

Painted accents

Though much maligned of late, there is no doubt that paint is one of the easiest ways to add character and theme to a garden with the minimum of expense. And if you change your mind, or change your garden's style, it is very easy to change your paint colour. A sunny yellow was chosen to paint the window frames, rear door and plant pots to link all together. This energetic colour was picked up in the achillea and the staining of yellow inside the white blooms of *Lilium regale*, injecting a sunny disposition to the garden even on a rainy day.

Crushed shell mulch

The side alley leading from the house into the garden was transformed into a part of the garden by the addition of a secondary boardwalk. All too often these areas are neglected, but if treated properly, these side alleys can form a bridging area between house and garden on first stepping outside. The light timber boardwalk glides into the main space over a mulch of reclaimed shell. This alludes to the common usage of boardwalks over beaches but also has a more practical use, forming a covering for a weedproof membrane. Shell mulches are becoming more readily available, bought by suppliers as a by-product of the fishing industry. Other companies use crushed cockleshells from managed sources. These are available in natural colours or with non-toxic, light-fast colour added to them.

This brick terrace makes the space feel larger and echoes the wall that wraps around the garden. A tall veil of *Verbena bonariensis* helps enclose the space.

PLANTS and PLANTING

An explosion of colour and height stopped the garden from becoming too flat, horizontal and easygoing. The varying heights within the planting and the inclusion of grasses also helped to separate areas. I had to keep in mind that the owners were novice gardeners, so nothing within the planting was to be too strictly ordered, difficult to grow or tricky to maintain. Grasses mixed with herbaceous perennials such as *Verbena bonariensis*, angelica, foxgloves and daylilies were used to playful effect. Massed in swathes through the beds, each would create its own climax of colour in order to gain the most attention. With closely planted spaces, a mixture of heights and spreads allows each plant to support the others.

Colours from the softer end of the hot colour scale were chosen in order that they might create a mix that was interesting but not clashing. Blooms would mix easily among the feathery flower-heads of grasses such as *Pennisetum aloepecuriodes* 'Hameln', *Miscanthus sinensis* 'Rotfuchs' and *Stipa gigantea*.

Around the hammock a jungle theme included plants such as banana, zantedeschia, bamboo and acanthus – large-leaved plants that would form a verdant zone highlighted here and there with understated flowers. All these plants were chosen not only for their architectural qualities but also for their hardy nature and minimal maintenance.

The flat, horizontal flower-heads of *Achillea* 'Walther Funcke' not only provide useful late summer colour but also associate perfectly with grasses.

Once discovered, reliable colourful groundcover is a real godsend and *Ajuga reptans* 'Catlin's Giant' is one of the best.

Achillea **'Walther Funcke'** (zones 3–8), also known as yarrow, is in fact a native of meadows, grassy places and hedgerows, so there is no surprise that it sits so well in almost any planting scheme. The traditional strident yellow plates of flower make themselves well known in flower borders, and new descendants of the common yarrow include many brightly coloured hybrids in an amazing array of hues, making this plant even more desirable. It grows well in any soil, even very impoverished ground, provided it is in full sun. The brick-red colouring of A. 'Walther Funcke' is particularly attractive; it fades to burnt orange with age, and each tiny flower has a bright mustard centre. It reaches a mid-height of 60cm (2ft) and has a long flowering period that makes it extremely useful in the small urban garden.

Ajuga reptans **'Catlin's Giant'** (zones 4–8) creeps on stoloniferous runners over the ground, quickly forming a dense groundcover of foliage with leaves up to 15cm (6in) long. It is so dense that it is almost impenetrable to weeds. The foliage of 'Catlin's Giant' is twice the size of the usual form, making it particularly useful in the front of a border or within a jungle scheme. However, it is not only the foliage that makes this plant an attractive border addition; late spring sees the purple-bronze mat of foliage give rise to a host of blue flower-spikes that bloom as well in shade as in sun (be aware that full sun all day may scorch the foliage). A. r. 'Catlin's Giant' is also very accommodating and will grow in almost any soil, even in poor ground.

While everybody knows that scent is a desirable garden asset, for those who are not sure how best to get it: try blocks of *Lilium regale* for starters.

Fargesia murielae is a delicate, frothy bamboo and with its bright green erectly upright canes, it is the perfect bamboo for hedging.

As a woodland plant, *Tellima grandiflora* makes perfect groundcover for shady spots, or planted at the front of borders in the shade of taller plants.

Lilium regale (zones 3–8) grows to a height of 1m (3ft) and has an exotic appearance. With its large trumpet blooms raised upon attractive glossy green foliage, it gives the impression that it could be difficult to grow, but nothing could be further from the truth. Planted in autumn in ground with plenty of sharp drainage added to it, *L. regale* is completely hardy and tolerates a wide range of conditions. It likes its base in shade, so it perhaps does best forcing its way through other plants to push up into sunshine. Try to emulate the conditions in this garden for the best effect. Here, in the still atmosphere, close to the walls in the sunniest spot of the garden, the air becomes still and warm, the walls radiating residual warmth to intensify the heady perfume of the evergreen jasmine and lilies well into the evening.

Fargesia murielae (zones 5–9) is not only useful as a living screen, but also as a backdrop to tropical planting. This is a particularly hardy bamboo that will survive in very low temperatures, making it a possibility for a wide range of gardeners. Like all fargesias, it does not have running rhizomes, usefully forming a good, evergreen clump that is easy to control. Grow it in fertile, moisture-retentive soil for the best results. Although *F. murielae* looks best when planted in semi-shade, it will tolerate full sun and wind. This bamboo requires little maintenance other than regular feeding (bamboo on the whole is a very hungry plant) and a thinning out from time to time. Its ultimate height is up to 4m (13ft) given ideal growing conditions.

Tellima grandiflora (zones 4–7), commonly known as fringe cups, prefers moist, humus-rich soil in partial shade, though it will grow in dry soil in full sun, even tolerating periods of drought. Evergreen, scalloped leaves smother out weeds to form an effective carpeting mass of pretty foliage. From late spring to midsummer, long racemes of tiny bell-shaped, greenish white flowers spring forth, reaching heights of up to 30cm (12in) above the foliage. Once introduced, numbers of this accommodating plant will soon bulk up due to its easy self-seeding nature. Its ultimate height is 80cm (32in) with a spread of 30cm (12in).

MODERN ALPINE GARDEN

In recent years there has been a resurgence of interest in scree beds – today's take on the rock gardens of the past. Using a single level of gravel as canvas, then washing low-growing colourful plants over the area, punctuated here and there with cobbles, a living piece of art is created. Scree beds provide a space-saving, low-maintenance garden with year-round interest whether viewed from above or at ground level. Accompanied by low-key landscaping, the scree bed takes centre stage to stunning effect.

PLANNING the GARDEN

Occasionally, a house is so dominant that its architectural style will dictate the garden's architecture. This was certainly true of the house here. The house together with its interior and exterior landscapes were designed to be linked together, with each space leading effortlessly into another. Huf houses are designed on Bauhaus principles using post-and-beam architecture. A timber frame supports load-bearing walls, allowing open-plan living with huge interior spaces. Floor-to-ceiling windows allow the maximum amount of light and look directly out on to the garden. The house is in a striking black and white design with a prominent split roof. Everything has a purpose and nothing is wasted within the space. This gives the building a unique yet timeless aesthetic, and I wanted the garden to reflect this.

At the back of the property, the garden is constantly on view. Seen through the large glass windows from both ground and first floor level, the garden had to provide vistas from both angles and have something of interest all year round.

It was important that I maintain a strong connection between house and garden and, with such strong materials used in the house, I wanted to use similar materials in the garden's construction. The signature colours of black and white (or as white as possible) would echo the property, and steel and dark timber would tie in with the architecture.

I decided to deal with the garden on two separate levels. When viewed as a whole, I wanted the garden to come together in a well-considered singular aesthetic; the space had to appear as simple as a modernist painting, each function (terrace, pathway, planting and so on) forming a

Planes of hard landscaping are effective when broken up with architectural detailing such as these cobbles. Linked colour tones cement the materials to each other.

confident addition of colour, shape, texture or form. The garden was treated as a blank canvas in which to arrange these elements, always keeping a strong relationship with the house. My time at the drawing board was crucial in an attempt to create a perpetual, dynamic, living piece of art.

When viewed from ground level, I wanted the space to be inviting and calm. Central to the whole space would be a large lawn that would be a year-round sea of green, viewed over a plane of gravel and cobbles, interspersed with low-growing alpines. This scree bed of gravel and cobbles would not distract from the overall ground-level vista but would court attention and closer inspection when seated upon the primary terrace leading straight out from the back of the house, or when one was seated on the lawn.

A second terrace was included in the warmest, sunniest section of the garden – the perfect place in which to admire both the beauty of the house and the more natural planting that softened the garden's edges with a wavering mass of meadow plants. Overall the garden's planting style would sweep from the height of tall, strong-growing herbaceous plants and grasses planted at the boundary edges down into the flat, ground-level lawn and alpines at the garden's centre. This would also have the effect of drawing the eye into the centre of the space.

Stainless steel features and light, airy flooring materials would add an injection of light and year-round interest, as well as structure and architectural ornament. However, these steel structures would not only be ornamental; they would also have a practical purpose, too.

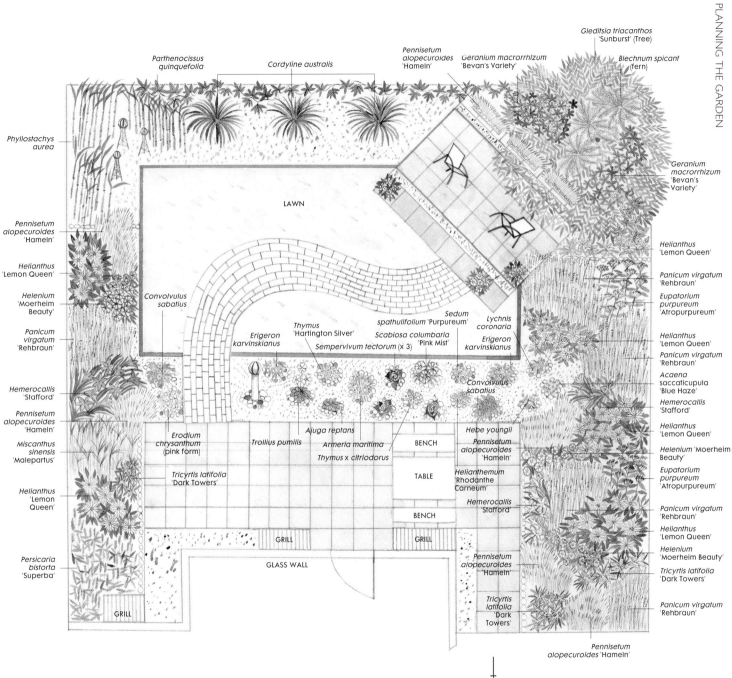

Parthenocissus quinquefolia

Cordyline australis

Pennisetum alopecuroides 'Hameln'

Geranium macrorrhizum 'Bevan's Variety'

Gleditsia triacanthos 'Sunburst' (Tree)

Blechnum spicant (fern)

Phyllostachys aurea

Geranium macrorrhizum 'Bevan's Variety'

LAWN

Pennisetum alopecuroides 'Hameln'

Helianthus 'Lemon Queen'

Helianthus 'Lemon Queen'

Helenium 'Moerheim Beauty'

Convolvulus sabatius

Panicum virgatum 'Rehbraun'

Panicum virgatum 'Rehbraun'

Eupatorium purpureum 'Atropurpureum'

Thymus 'Hartington Silver'

Sedum spathulifolium 'Purpureum'

Lychnis coronaria

Helianthus 'Lemon Queen'

Erigeron karvinskianus

Scabiosa columbaria 'Pink Mist'

Erigeron karvinskianus

Panicum virgatum 'Rehbraun'

Sempervivum tectorum (x 3)

Hemerocallis 'Stafford'

Acaena saccaticupula 'Blue Haze'

Convolvulus sabatius

Hemerocallis 'Stafford'

Pennisetum alopecuroides 'Hameln'

Helianthus 'Lemon Queen'

Erodium chrysanthum (pink form)

Ajuga reptans

Hebe youngii

Miscanthus sinensis 'Malepartus'

Trollius pumilis

Armeria maritima

BENCH

Pennisetum alopecuroides 'Hameln'

Helenium 'Moerheim Beauty'

Thymus x citriodorus

TABLE

Helianthemum 'Rhodanthe Carneum'

Eupatorium purpureum 'Atropurpureum'

Tricyrtis latifolia 'Dark Towers'

Helianthus 'Lemon Queen'

Hemerocallis 'Stafford'

BENCH

Panicum virgatum 'Rehbraun'

Helianthus 'Lemon Queen'

GRILL

GRILL

Helianthus 'Lemon Queen'

Helenium 'Moerheim Beauty'

Pennisetum alopecuroides 'Hameln'

Persicaria bistorta 'Superba'

GLASS WALL

Tricyrtis latifolia 'Dark Towers'

GRILL

Tricyrtis latifolia 'Dark Towers'

Panicum virgatum 'Rehbraun'

Pennisetum alopecuroides 'Hameln'

N

Garden area: 11m (36ft) long x 12.5m (41ft) wide

SPECIAL FEATURES

With so much of the garden on view for so much of the year, it was important that it was the essence of pared down simplicity. I decided to use a limited palette of materials to maximize the visual impact of this garden. This simplicity would also allow the garden to be 'read' from any given angle – important in a home with so many windows.

Lawn

The main colour in the garden was going to be a green swathe of lawn, and I wanted a broad, generous area to form a backdrop or frame for the other garden features that would be set around this central focus. A generous rectangle of grass was set within a 10 × 10cm (4 × 4in) timber strip painted deep black in order to echo the timber construction of the house. This simple detail gave an effective finish to the lawn, with the black edging visually acting as the lawn's frame, particularly effective when seen from the first floor above. The symmetry of the lawn had to be 100 per cent correct; any corners that were not exactly 90° would be glaringly obvious from the elevated position of the balcony. The principles of a 3–4–5 triangle were used to ensure these corners were exact. The strip also acted as a mowing edge, which was to become particularly useful when a thick gravel mulch was laid next to the lawn to form the main planting bed as loose stones could very easily damage lawnmower blades. This strip separated the two areas, making the grass easy to grow and maintain as well as cutting down on maintenance.

As the lawn was to be the centre of attention, it was necessary that we lay as high a quality of sward as possible. If you are looking for equally good-quality turf, use a specialist supplier rather than buy from a local garden centre. Turf will be available in a variety of grades at a variety of prices.

Path

Paths are the arteries of any garden: they provide the means to walk around a space to see what lies within it; they keep your feet dry after a downpour; and should form a non-slip route around the space. You should always treat any paths with the same attention as you might your terrace, patio or indeed flowerbeds.

To create a feeling of movement, both visually and physically, the central path needed to form a bold statement, creating a confident sweep dissecting the lawn. A small, modular paving unit would add to the feeling of adventure, creating the illusion of added space and making it easier to form a curve than it would be

In strictly practical terms, paths simply form access routes linking various areas of the garden together. In reality, however, they do a great deal more. Paths create journeys and adventures through a garden, so they need to be as attractive and interesting as possible to invite you to explore.

Do not add furniture to a garden as an afterthought. Make sure that you link it to your garden's overall style so that it complements and adds to the visual appeal of your space.

using large pieces of paving slab. This is a common design trick in the small garden. Large paving slabs tend to eat into visual space, but the smaller the unit size, the greater the number of units and therefore the greater the illusion of space.

Texture was also an important consideration to ensure that the path (particularly with its light utilitarian colour) would not become visually bland. However, it proved impossible to source a paving product with the colour and texture I wanted; surfacing materials just did not have the degree of roughness I was looking for. I therefore decided to use a walling product instead. With a rough textured finish, light colour and small modular unit size, this product provided me with texture, a non-slip finish, a linking colour and flexibility. So all my criteria were met. Although the product manufacturer would understandably not guarantee such a product when not used for its original purpose, the walling units were frost-proof and, as foot traffic in the garden was sure to be light, it was bound to be satisfactory. This use proved most successful – unusual but not outlandish, strong but not domineering, practical but attractive. As a light textured surface, it hit the spot as far as I was concerned.

Terrace

On occasion, reconstituted utility concrete slabs seem entirely appropriate to an area. Indeed, cheaper utility slabs have a modern industrial feel that can work perfectly within the urban garden, particularly when attached to such a modern property. The slabs we used for both the primary and smaller secondary terraces had a slightly riven surface to emulate the natural qualities of stone and make them non-slip. The terrace straight outside the large sliding glass doors at the rear of the property was joined to a gravel garden of alpine plants. I wanted to create a thematic link with the secondary terrace, so a gap was left at both front and rear of the secondary terrace and in-filled with loose Scottish pebbles to create an interesting ornamental detail and link the two terraces together visually.

Scree bed

Both a garden feature and a specialist horticultural growing medium for a particular group of plants, scree gardens combine rock garden and true alpine plants to form a low-growing, easy-to-maintain tapestry of plants. Their diminutive stature makes rock plants very suitable for the small modern garden where a large collection can be grown in a relatively small space. Their ease of care has seen an increase in their popularity. This scree garden was sited directly outside the huge wall of glass the main living area, in an open sunny position. A long, wide run given over completely to rock plants ensured a generous scale and considerable impact, with these small-stature plants inviting closer inspection.

The main consideration in construction was to try to emulate the natural well-drained growing conditions of the original habitat of this group of alpine plants. Digging in large quantities of sharp sand and grit was imperative, then once planted a top dressing of chipped stone or gravel was used. Gravel not only forms an attractive and natural setting for alpine and rock plants, but it also encourages good drainage, thereby preventing rotting-off around the collar of the plants, discouraging weeds, conserving moisture and protecting the soil's surface from compaction from heavy rain or even watering. Cobbles provided additional interest and were placed randomly here and there to form visual punctuation. They are also useful for discouraging people from walking over the area and causing instant devastation to the design and the planting.

Ornamentation

Well-chosen garden accessories are the final adornments that bring a garden to life; they are the decorative accents that personalize a space, and as such can make or break an overall look. Think carefully about the containers, obelisks and furniture you use in your garden; mixing materials or styles will create an untidy disjointed space. Instead, co-ordinate your accessories to that they complement the theme of the garden. Stainless steel was used in this space to repeat the steel used in the building, adding to the

Whether used to support climbing plants or purely to add architectural interest to your borders, obelisks add an upward thrust of energy and make the most of valuable vertical space in the small urban garden.

The soothing, musical qualities of water can be brought into any urban garden, no matter how small. Here, a steel water feature adds visual interest within the main gravel bed as well as providing a beautiful trickling sound.

Containers highlight
favourite plants that are
key to your planting
scheme. Available in
numerous materials, shapes
and sizes, think about what
your pots will add to the
space as a whole. Here, a
row of steel troughs allows
for greater quantities of
feature plants, while their
length enhances the width of
the secondary terrace.

sophisticated simplicity, clean lines and overall urban style. Steel adds light, reflection and modernism to this garden, too. And though steel is costly, it is a definite investment as it will never rust or degrade. All the ornamental features used in this garden were not fixed so that if the owners move they can take them all with them.

Water feature

This was a space that needed water. Soothing and cooling, I wanted a feature from which a trickle could be heard anywhere in the garden, and also within the house on a hot day, when the great expanses of glass wall would slide open.

However, I didn't want the feature to dominate. A simple self-circulating sump system would be easy to maintain, and with an overall height of roughly 1m (3ft) would be in proportion to the scale of the alpine bed where it was to be sited. I chose this location because the gravel bed would give the impression of a dry waterbed, echoing aspects of *karesansui*, the Japanese craft of dry landscape where each cobble and stone has its place in re-creating an imaginary watercourse. Here, there would be the interesting juxtaposition of the west-facing border of sun-loving alpines that grow in dry soil with the water feature in close proximity.

How to install a sump water system

Available in kit form, self-circulating water features are exceptionally easy to install. All of the materials you need will be included in the kit. However, you will need an electrician to

install a power supply to power the pump for your water feature. A circular plastic pre-formed pond shell, which holds water and permanently houses your pump, will need to be buried below ground level. Use a spirit level to make sure the edges are level once it is in the ground. If not, water will spill out at the edges, depleting the water supply and potentially leading to burn-out of the pump's motor.

Next, place the pump in the pond shell, balancing it on some bricks if it needs extra height to bring it to its final level, then add the spout, fountain or feature from which the water will spill.

Pond kits usually include a plastic cover or grill to support a camouflaging layer of slate chips, gravel or pebbles. Before covering this layer, ensure your stones are clean and grit-free. Dirt could potentially damage your pump.

Finally, fill your sump with water to the top (this will self-circulate) and then switch on the power. In hot weather, regularly top up the water supply as warm weather or wind can lead to rapid evaporation.

Right A house with strong architectural features requires the garden's hard landscaping to be well defined if it is not to play second fiddle. A mix of meadow plants at the garden's periphery softens the edges.

Left Simple touches such as collected pebbles and stones add personality to a space, evoking memories and truly making the garden your own.

PLANTS and PLANTING

Though herbaceous perennials mixed with some shrub material were used at the garden's edges and within containers, the main emphasis in this garden was upon the low-growing alpine plants. Recycling the 1970s notion of a rock garden, this retro feature was brought up to date with the use of gravel and cobbles on one continuous flat plane. The architecture of the house was certainly strong enough to accommodate a strong design statement, so once we had created ideal planting conditions with thorough soil conditioning, planting began in earnest.

Grown for its tight rosettes of foliage, *Sedum spathulifolium* 'Purpureum' forms ground-hugging mats of colour. Mix alpine sedums together to form an interesting tapestry of succulent leaf sprinkled in summer with the almost unexpected addition of brightly coloured flowers.

Sedum spathulifolium **'Purpureum'** (zones 5–9), or stonecrop, has neat and appealing foliage that is very useful in the rock or scree garden. Equally attractive grown in raised troughs, containers or beds, it provides texture, colour and shape. Most stonecrops require full sun, but S.s. 'Purpureum' tolerates light shade. Reaching an overall height of 10cm (4in), this plant will quickly spread to 60cm (2ft), producing a bright yellow haze of starry flowers borne above fleshy leaves in midsummer. Highlighting these fascinating low growers by growing them in raised troughs, planters or pots lifts them up towards the eye, making them easier to enjoy. The genus *Sedum* consists of over 400 varieties of plants and all are easily propagated by stem or root cuttings. Handle them carefully, however – all parts can cause stomach upsets if ingested and the sap can sometimes irritate skin.

Erigeron karvinskianus is an unpretentious, simple and whimsical addition to the rock garden.

The full, feathery flower-heads of *Pennisetum alopecuroides* dance when caught in a breeze, perfect for adding some playful movement to your borders.

Sempervivum tectorum is among a host of plants from which stem many traditional beliefs. As far back as the Roman Empire, it was grown on roofs to protect against thunder, pestilence and fire.

Erigeron karvinskianus (zones 9–10), also known as wall daisy, requires sharp drainage, sunshine and not too much winter wet to grow well. This carpeting, vigorous perennial flowers profusely all summer long, each yellow-centred flower-head opening white and fading through pink and violet. Though suited to the rock garden, the wall daisy does very well planted in cracks in paving or in walls, so it is perfect for the cottage garden, too. Treated well, although this daisy may only reach 15–30cm (6–12in) in height, it will spread to 1m (3ft 3in) or more.

Pennisetum alopecuroides (zones 5–9), or fountain grass, was planted in containers to distract a little from the straight edges of the hard landscaping. Its flowers open in summer through autumn – fat bristles of purple-tinged spikelets borne upon long stems above a mass of arching foliage. As the season progresses, the spikelets fade to a blur of silvery buff, adding much to the early winter plant scene. Well-drained soil in sun is the requirement for the strong growth of this plant, and maintenance is limited to a comb with the fingers in spring and a good mulch to see the plant through the winter in frost-prone areas. Its ultimate height is 60–150cm (2–5 ft), with a spread of 60–120cm (2–4ft).

Sempervivum tectorum (zones 8–11), or houseleeks, will tolerate spartan conditions. Open rosettes of foliage reminiscent of cabbages rather than leeks reach up to 10cm (4in) across. The foliage is a fleshy, blue-green in colour and often stained red-purple. Otherworldly stems bear pink-purple star-shaped flowers in midsummer from the centre of each rosette. Make use of the conditions in which sempervivum will grow and plant it into garden walls, which it will bring, quite literally, to life. Plants reach a height of 15cm (6in) and a spread of 50cm (20in).

If you have ever battled with pernicious bindweed in your garden, you may be tempted to give *Convolvulus sabatius*, bindweed's cousin, a wide berth. However, this would be a mistake.

The ferny soft, silvery foliage of *Erodium chrysanthum* (pink form) forms a dense, tufted mound – a useful shape on the flat plane of a scree garden.

A great groundcover plant, *Acaena saccaticulpula* 'Blue Haze' will quickly cover large areas with its ground-hugging carpet of silvery-blue foliage.

Convolvulus sabatius (zones 8–11) has trumpet-shaped blooms of pale to deep lavender-blue hovering just above the foliage from midsummer well into autumn. This plant forms a useful, beautiful blue mat to the garden's floor. It is unfussy with regard to soil, growing well in both impoverished and healthy ground. However, it does detest the wet. Well-drained soil is an absolute necessity, and a warm site with lots of sunshine will be appreciated, too. This plant is not completely hardy; top growth will almost certainly be killed by winter frosts, but as the spring warms the garden up, you will find that shoots appear from below the plant in much the same way as with a fuchsia. This plant will reach only a diminutive 15cm (6in) in height, but will spread to cover 45cm (18in) on the ground.

Erodium chrysanthum (pink form) (zones 5–9) gives rise to a host of sprays of delicate pale pink blooms that continue all summer long. To get the best from this small perennial, grow it in gritty, humus-rich soil that is sharply drained, and position it in full sun; a rock, gravel or scree garden provides the perfect conditions for it to thrive. Fully hardy, this plant is pest- and trouble-free, its only aversion being to excessive winter wet. If it looks like you are in for a rainy spell, provide it with some protection. The ultimate height of this plant is 15cm (6in) and its spread is 40cm (16in)

Acaena saccaticulpula 'Blue Haze' (zones 5–9) may be small in stature but lacks nothing in vigour, quickly spreading when given favourable conditions. The New Zealand burr, as it is commonly known, will only reach 8cm (3in) in height. The blue-grey of the foliage makes *A.s.* 'Blue Haze' very distinctive from other acaena varieties. Summer sees copper-brown to red burrs of flower flecked over the surface of the foliage, but unlike most flowers, these blooms do not detract from the foliage that makes this plant so desirable. It looks very well in the gravel garden, but also in between stepping stones, in planting pockets within a terrace or cascading over a wall or the lip of a container. Grow *A.s.* 'Blue Haze' in moderately fertile, well-drained soil in full sun, simply pulling up stems at will if the plant grows too enthusiastically.

Hebe 'Youngii' lends evergreen permanence to the scree or rock garden, forming low-growing mounds of foliage that are extremely valuable in the winter garden.

Rock roses like this *Helianthemum* 'Rhodanthe Carneum' have always been popular in scree beds and rock gardens, valued for their neat habit, attractive foliage and brilliantly coloured flowers.

Fragrant, delicate and spreading, *Thymus* 'Hartington Silver' looks great in an alpine garden, between paving slabs and in herb gardens.

Hebe 'Youngii' (zones 8–9) is an attractive plant; the tiny evergreen leaves are shiny mid-green, each edged with red and held on dark brown, near-black stems. Summer heightens the beauty of this hebe, giving rise to racemes of large white-throated violet flowers. These evergreen shrubs need sun, protection from drying winds and good drainage in order to thrive, reaching 20 × 60cm (8 × 24in) when mature. Hebes are a good addition to the year-round structure of scree and rock gardens but also look good in containers on the terrace and planted in blocks through the border, where they will create considerable impact.

Helianthemum 'Rhodanthe Carneum' (zones 5–7) has attractive silver-grey leaves that, in warmer areas, will last through the winter, particularly if plants are given a deep winter mulch. Late spring to early summer sees the arrival of pale pink flowers, each roughly 2.5cm (1in) across and flushed yellow at the centre. Though each bloom only lasts a day, a good summer will provide blooms in such abundance that they smother the foliage almost completely. Trim the shrub back after blooming in order to keep the plant in shape as well as promote strong new growth and encourage a second flush of flower in late summer. Fertile, moist, well-drained soil in sun will encourage *H.* 'Rhodanthe Carneum' to reach its largest size of 30 × 45cm (12 × 18in).

Thymus 'Hartington Silver' (zones 5–8) is an easy-to-grow variety of thyme, of which there are over 350 species to choose from. *T.* 'Hartington Silver' is best grown in well-drained, neutral to alkaline soil in full sun, where it will produce a thick cover of dark green leaves edged with cream, followed by tiny lavender flowers in spring and summer. Space plants 30cm (12in) apart in order to create a low undulating mound along a pathway or at the edge of the scree, rock or herb garden. Though *T.* 'Hartington Silver' is drought tolerant, do water it in well, particularly in dry summers, and cut it back after flowering to maintain a tight shape. This hardy perennial reaches 2.5–5cm (1–2in) in height.

FAMILY GARDEN

This space was to be a gloriously natural, stimulating and fun family garden. The brief was to inspire the imaginations of the children while allowing sufficient space for adults to entertain. Nothing was to be out of bounds or too tidy – a striped lawn was simply out of the question. This family garden needed to be safe for the youngsters to play and explore without rules, and a space to lift the spirits of adults. Unfussy and uncomplicated, it should be a welcoming place in which to leave the rest of the world behind.

PLANNING the GARDEN

For this family the kitchen is the heart of the house and they wanted to extend this living space out into the garden. Any new terracing was to be an extension of this already well-used space, an outside area where the family could spend time together and entertain friends. The children use the conservatory as a play room, so the garden would always be on full view, hopefully luring them outside to an extended play area. With such an emphasis on linking the garden and house together, it was important to get the terrace outside the back door just right. It should be large and inviting but not overpowering, and integrate perfectly into the garden as a whole; the material chosen would be pivotal in making the scheme work.

A large play area was obligatory, but we all felt that too often children's play equipment can dominate a space. The children had almost outgrown their plastic swing set, but still loved it. Their well-loved 'sky-seat' was to be re-incorporated into a new timber play frame with new, larger swing seats and a slide. In order to keep the garden as naturally green as possible, bamboo was chosen as a living screen. We planted ten *Phyllostachys nigra* plants in two groups, successfully disguising the large area of play equipment. These clump-forming bamboos will reach heights of 4m (13ft) given the right conditions, providing movement and sound to the garden as well as handy canes for plant supports. Do not worry if your bamboo produces green canes at first; it takes a couple of seasons for the canes to become a deep, lustrous black.

Before the redesign, the rear garden was simply a large lawn reaching all the way up to the rear of the house, which though dull, did make the space seem big. It was important to try to retain this open feeling as far as possible but to add interest to it. I decided to divide the space into sections, each area merging into the next through a slight overlap; a liberal veiling of plants would also ease the transition. Repeating the plants used would also create linkage. This would perhaps remain unnoticed, but would tie the space together in a subliminal way. Repeating motif plants is a key technique in moving the garden user around and through a space, making the journey around the garden a friendly experience.

A large lawn would be central to the garden, providing a soft surface to accommodate play. However, this area needed a focus that would distract the children from simply bypassing the area and heading straight for the fun of the swings and slide or the privacy of the play house. In such close proximity to the terrace, whatever we chose would be in full view. A living willow igloo complete with tunnel was chosen that would become a living sculpture – a talking point for the adults and an interesting den for the children.

As far as plants were concerned, though the clients love being outside and are not averse to a little pottering, they are not wildly keen gardeners themselves. However, they wanted to steer clear of the traditional low-maintenance evergreen shrubberies. I took on the challenge to hook their interest in gardening by using bright, vibrant plants that would attract their eye and create enthusiasm, unwittingly creating the desire to nurture these plants that bring so much pleasure. Seasonal interest would also help, so that the garden would remain enjoyable throughout the year and would not be ignored in winter.

Gardens are not just for the grown-ups. A successful garden considers the requirements of everyone who will use the space.

FAMILY
GARDEN

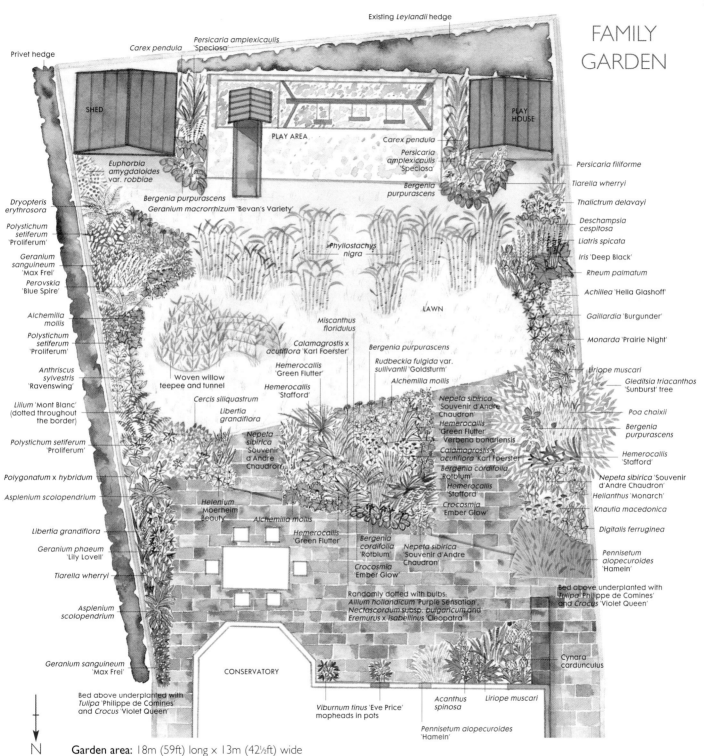

Existing *Leylandii* hedge

Persicaria amplexicaulis
'Speciosa'

Carex pendula

Privet hedge

SHED

PLAY AREA

PLAY
HOUSE

Carex pendula

Persicaria amplexicaulis
'Speciosa'

*Bergenia
purpurascens*

Persicaria filiforme

Tiarella wherryi

*Euphorbia
amygdaloides
var. robbiae*

Bergenia purpurascens
Geranium macrorrhizum 'Bevan's Variety'

Thalictrum delavayi

*Dryopteris
erythrosora*

*Deschampsia
cespitosa*

*Polystichum
setiferum
'Proliferum'*

*Phyllostachys
nigra*

Liatris spicata

Iris 'Deep Black'

*Geranium
sanguineum
'Max Frei'*

Rheum palmatum

*Perovskia
'Blue Spire'*

LAWN

Achillea 'Hella Glashoff'

*Alchemilla
mollis*

*Miscanthus
floridulus*

Gaillardia 'Burgunder'

*Polystichum
setiferum
'Proliferum'*

*Calamagrostis x
acutiflora* 'Karl Foerster'

Bergenia purpurascens

Monarda 'Prairie Night'

*Hemerocallis
'Green Flutter'*

Rudbeckia fulgida var.
sullivantii 'Goldsturm'

Liriope muscari

*Anthriscus
sylvestris
'Ravenswing'*

Woven willow
teepee and tunnel

*Hemerocallis
'Stafford'*

Alchemilla mollis

*Gleditsia triacanthos
'Sunburst' tree*

Lilium 'Mont Blanc'
(dotted throughout
the border)

Cercis siliquastrum

*Libertia
grandiflora*

*Nepeta sibirica
'Souvenir d'Andre
Chaudron'*

Poa chaixii

*Hemerocallis
'Green Flutter'*

*Bergenia
purpurascens*

*Polystichum setiferum
'Proliferum'*

*Nepeta
sibirica
'Souvenir
d'Andre
Chaudron'*

Verbena bonariensis

*Calamagrostis x
acutiflora* 'Karl Foerster'

*Hemerocallis
'Stafford'*

Polygonatum x hybridum

*Bergenia cordifolia
'Rotblum'*

Nepeta sibirica 'Souvenir
d'Andre Chaudron'

Asplenium scolopendrium

*Helenium
'Moerheim
Beauty'*

*Hemerocallis
'Stafford'*

Helianthus 'Monarch'

*Crocosmia
'Ember Glow'*

Knautia macedonica

Libertia grandiflora

Alchemilla mollis

Digitalis ferruginea

*Geranium phaeum
'Lily Lovell'*

*Hemerocallis
'Green Flutter'*

*Bergenia
cordifolia
'Rotblum'*

*Nepeta sibirica
'Souvenir d'Andre
Chaudron'*

*Pennisetum
alopecuroides
'Hameln'*

Tiarella wherryi

*Crocosmia
'Ember Glow'*

*Asplenium
scolopendrium*

Bed above underplanted with
Tulipa 'Philippe de Comines'
and *Crocus* 'Violet Queen'

Randomly dotted with bulbs:
Allium hollandicum 'Purple Sensation',
Nectascordum subsp. *bulgaricum* and
Eremurus x isabellinus 'Cleopatra'

*Cynara
cardunculus*

*Geranium sanguineum
'Max Frei'*

CONSERVATORY

Bed above underplanted with
Tulipa 'Philippe de Comines'
and *Crocus* 'Violet Queen'

Viburnum tinus 'Eve Price'
mopheads in pots

*Acanthus
spinosa*

Liriope muscari

*Pennisetum alopecuroides
'Hameln'*

N

Garden area: 18m (59ft) long x 13m (42½ft) wide

SPECIAL FEATURES

It was important that all the features in the garden would be able to take the knocks that the children would throw at them, without detracting from the soft, natural look of the garden overall. Anything that would not sit well in the tranquil environment of the garden would be excluded, but it was still necessary to include some bulky play equipment. Though all the features would seem relatively large in the confines of a fairly small backyard, the challenge was to ensure that any potentially dominating feature would be screened or toned down so that all of the features would interconnect to form a harmonious whole.

Slate terrace

Inevitably, the terrace is visually the hardest of structures in any garden; its purpose is to be tough and strong enough to support quantities of foot traffic, furniture and various other structures. Here, the terrace would act as a diving board from which the rest of the garden would emanate. As an expensive investment, indeed the most expensive cost within the garden, it was essential that the chosen material and the terrace itself would stand the test of time both practically and aesthetically. It was essential to choose wisely or the whole process could become a costly mistake.

The clients had already laid their kitchen floor in a hardwearing slate, so it made perfect sense to use this material externally, linking interior and exterior effortlessly. Like almost all natural stones, slate is ageless. It splits easily along its planes, giving it a rustic appearance that complements other building materials as well as the unrefined, natural qualities of soil and plants.

To give the terrace a strong dynamic and to create additional interest, I decided to cut the edge of the terrace on the diagonal; this axis would form a step leading down to a large central planting bed and two extended step treads, cut on the opposite diagonal, would lead casually into the garden beyond or could be used as secondary seating areas in their own right. Although this bisection forms slashes through the space, it is a valuable design element that prevents the terrace from becoming too staid.

Above Hardwearing slate was a natural choice for the terrace and created continuity with the slate floor indoors.

Right A living igloo woven from green willow ensures a degree of integration between play equipment and the garden as a whole.

Willow igloo and tunnel

A traditional material that ties us to our rural past, willow is flexible, attractive and easily woven. Willow structures are sculptural and ornamental, made from an environmentally sustainable crop that is perfect for the natural garden. The structure was also designed to entice children to play. Green willow is extremely easy to manipulate and it is the simplest structures that work best. Willow weaving is truly a pleasure, connecting you with the past, and is also a very quick process – just a day's work can produce amazing results of which you will undoubtedly feel proud.

However, while the only limit to the type of structure you make is your imagination, the time within which you can build it is more limited. You can only obtain living willow through the winter months when the sap is down, so make sure you place an order with your supplier well in advance and allocate a window of time in your diary for construction. The willow will need planting almost as soon as it arrives. If there will be an unavoidable delay between arrival and planting, then stand the willow upright in water or heel it into the ground until you are ready to get weaving.

First, consider the siting of your structure. Contrary to popular belief, willow does not need excessively wet ground in order to thrive; it survives quite happily in the same conditions as other trees and shrubs. An open, sunny site where the ground is well cultivated and weed-free is ideal. Provided the rods are pushed into the ground to a depth of around 15cm (6in) where they will quickly develop roots, the open, flexible nature of your willow structure will allow it to withstand considerable winds.

The willow igloo that I constructed required about 30 upright willows and 60 weavers to secure and tie the structure together. It was a simple process, working in a circle with the live end of willows pushed into the ground around the circumference at intervals of about 20cm (8in). These were simply bent together at the top and tied centrally, with weavers woven around the structure to keep the whole solid. Willow tends to be bushier at the top than the bottom, so additional shorter lengths were placed at the igloo's base in order to

At the bottom of the garden a secret play house allows children the privacy they so enjoy. Miniature planting beds at each side of the entrance encourage an interest in all things growing and green.

bush out the bottom with foliage, too. The tunnel leading into the igloo was built following
the same construction method to provide even more fun and adventure for the children.

Any living willow structure needs to thicken up over its first year, and any unruly growths
simply woven back in. In successive growing seasons the willow will be much stronger, so you
will need to give the whole thing a 'haircut' occasionally.

Play equipment

If we are to entice youngsters away from computer games and television out into the
garden, then a swing, slide or climbing frame is almost a necessity. If your budget allows,
choose timber products to blend more easily into your space.

Here, a screen of living bamboo was planted to mask the children from the 'prying'
eyes of adults – an inviting prospect for a growing child. A degree of privacy is important
to children, making them feel independent and enhancing their learning experience. For
this reason, the play house at the bottom of the garden was given its own meandering path
through planting to would allow private play. It was hoped that the surrounding bed would
also encourage the children to develop an interest in plants, and perhaps even to grow a
few of their own favourites.

The planting had a variety of roles to play within the space. Many clients with children understandably want to retain as large a lawn as possible and, while this is a practical requirement, the decision can be at the cost of the planting – large lawns inevitably mean small borders. However, although the plants wrap around the peripheries of this space, I did not want them to go unnoticed. Bright colours colliding against one another in an energetic display would ensure they would not be overlooked. This exuberant display is made more harmonious with a scattering of grasses to frame the colours in the foreground and lightly screen garden structures in the background.

Though largely herbaceous, many of the plants will have a winter presence against the strong backdrop of evergreen bamboo and the outlined silhouettes of the two existing trees that were incorporated into the space. All the plants are reasonably low maintenance, though all herbaceous planting requires an element of care (mostly weeding) within its first couple of seasons.

Summer brings with it not only energetic colour, but also lots of wildlife feasting upon the abundance of blooms. Combined with the presence of lively children, this natural and laidback garden has a definite zing.

Psychedelic colours make each flower-head reverberate and fizz. *Helenium* 'Moerheim Beauty' is an exciting border plant that looks great mingled with late summer grasses.

Helenium 'Moerheim Beauty' (zones 3–9) is a lively addition to the summer border, with its prominent central cone of brown dusted darkest gold, and swept back petals ranging from dark coppery red through russet with random flecks of gold. Plant it in autumn in deep, rich soil and mulch your new plants well to guarantee the best displays. Flowering throughout the summer and into early autumn, blooms are held upon long stems, making them ideal as cut flowers. Reaching up to 1.2m (4ft) in height, heleniums may require propping with plant supports or (a more attractive option) pea sticks if they are not supported by surrounding plants.

Plants that bloom over long periods are essential in the urban garden where every scrap of space has to count. The sensational blooms and long flowering season of *Hemerocallis* 'Green Flutter' make it a must-have plant.

Hemerocallis 'Green Flutter' (zones 3–9), or day lily, lacks nothing in terms of impact, blooming throughout mid- to late summer. Although each bloom lasts for just a day, there are many successive flowers. Large light yellow blooms rise above evergreen strap-shaped leaves to a height of 50cm (20in). Plant it in front of winter-flowering shrubs where it will be shown to its best advantage. A true curio, *H.* 'Green Flutter' bears nocturnal blooms; its flowers open in mid-afternoon and last throughout the night. Growing well in sun and light shade, an annual feed is the only maintenance it require to keep flowering freely.

Willow has long been valued for its pliability, making it perfect for weaving into structures, baskets and sculpture. The only limit to what you can create with *Salix viminalis* is your imagination.

Rudbeckia fulgida var. *sullivantii* 'Goldsturm' has bold and brassy flower-heads. Give this plant centre stage in your autumn border – it will try to grab all the attention anyway.

In recent years the true benefits of grasses such as *Calamagrostis* x *acutiflora* 'Karl Foerster' have been embraced by the gardener.

Salix viminalis (zones 4–8) has a fast growth rate that makes it the perfect willow variety for building living structures; even year-old rods produce attractive dense fresh growth. However, it is controllable. If your structure becomes a little shaggy after its first year, prune errant straggly whips or weave them back into the original structure in order to retain the original shape. You will find it immensely tolerant, too. It can withstand wet, heavy soils, cold winds and salty coastlines, making it perfect for any garden.

Rudbeckia fulgida var. *sullivantii* 'Goldsturm' (zones 3–9) has narrow golden yellow petals that radiate out from a central cone of dark brown from late summer to mid-autumn. This variety produces larger flower-heads than most of the species – up to 12cm (5in) wide – but sacrifices width for height. It reaches 60cm (2ft) in height but blooms with such profusion that you will be tricked into thinking of it as a much more statuesque plant. It is a perfect bridge in the flower garden, filling the lull between summer and autumn that so often occurs in gardens. Divide it every two years to promote healthy sturdy plants.

Calamagrostis x *acutiflora* 'Karl Foerster' (zones 5–9) is one of the first grasses of the year to bloom, stiffly upright, with heather-purple heads that slowly bleach in the sun to a straw colour as autumn approaches. This tall grass reaches a height of 1.8m (6ft), so it is useful as a buffer plant, forming a backdrop and frame to the hot flower colours of late summer. Although this plant is happy to play second fiddle, it has an important role because primary players would be lessened dramatically without it. Use it to semi-screen views, as a veiling transitionary plant between planting styles in a Mediterranean garden or to provide a visual breathing space in the packed cottage garden.

You just cannot believe your luck on first encountering *Gaillardia* x *grandiflora* 'Burgunder' – this plant just will not stop flowering.

So many of us fall for the charms of foxgloves, but you do not have to keep them in the shade. Varieties such as *Digitalis ferruginea* will happily put up with sunshine, so scatter them throughout your garden.

Persicaria amplexicaulis 'Speciosa' is an extremely useful plant: reliable, unfussy and attractive.

Gaillardia x *grandiflora* 'Burgunder' (zones 3–9) has deep-red, daisy-like flowers that make this plant most appealing in a hot border or gravel garden. Reaching a mid-height of about 50cm (20in), it has unbelievable stamina, flowering from early summer to early autumn. However, keep an eye on it because it can be short-lived, so cut it back to around 15cm (6in) in late summer to encourage new basal growth that survives frost well.

Digitalis ferruginea (zones 4–8), commonly known as the rusty foxglove, is a robust perennial that rises from a neat rosette of dark green, glossy leaves. Towering spires of miniature coppery yellow trumpets, each streaked with brown veins, erupt from the border in midsummer, reaching heights of 1.5m (5ft) in their second year. Reliably self-supporting, foxgloves look spectacular *en masse*, becoming tall towers for bees to buzz through and around. Though they will undoubtedly self-seed, to ensure you increase your stocks, collect the seed from your plants in late autumn when the seed-heads have dried out by shaking upturned flower-spikes into a paper bag, and sow seed in a cold frame the following spring.

Persicaria amplexicaulis 'Speciosa' (zones 5–9) is an amazingly garden-worthy plant. It grows strongly without complaint in almost any soil and aspect, forming a mass of attractive foliage and flowers. Each bloom, held on a long stalk, is a narrow 10cm (4in) long spike that blooms bright deep red from midsummer until it is quelled by the first frosts. Allow it some space to flex its muscles and it will be a reliable plant clumping to a height and spread of 1.2m (4ft).

Liatris spicata 'Blazing Star' is one of those retro plants that has made a comeback. It looks great when successfully combined with grasses and other late-flowering perennials.

The ubiquitous *Alchemilla mollis* is endlessly useful in any garden. It is a plant that we never tire of, faithfully reliable with an understated beauty.

Monarda 'Prairie Night' looks great in the informal flower garden, growing steadily into tall, aromatic, self-supporting plants.

Liatris spicata 'Blazing Star' (zones 3–8) seems to be magnetic to bees and butterflies, so it is a must-have in the wildlife garden. Strangely, the flowers open upon a spike from top to bottom. These pink-purple, long-lasting flowers make this plant popular for cut flowers. If you grow it in light, not-too-fertile soil (it is often incorporated into meadow plantings) and keep it moist, it will bloom in summer to a height of 60cm (24in).

Alchemilla mollis (zones 3–8), or lady's mantle, is invaluable in all types of gardens – traditional, modern, courtyard or nature. Sumptuous rounded velvety leaves catch the early morning dew or raindrops after a light shower, each bead forming a metallic ball-bearing that glistens jewel-like. With minimum maintenance, lady's mantle self-seeds at whim, looking at home wherever it pops up, and the sulphuric acid-yellow flowers form a fabulous foam of colour in early summer. It has an ultimate height and spread of 30cm (12in).

Monarda 'Prairie Night' (zones 4–9) has unusual bracts of long-lasting two-toned blooms that will be buzzing with bees and butterflies all summer. The leaves arrive first, a deliciously scented preliminary of foliage before a deluge of flower. *M*. 'Prairie Night' is a firework of sweet-scented purple that, once flowering is over, provides a useful winter silhouette. Monarda is prone to mildew, from either too much wet or sometimes from too dry an environment. *M*. 'Prairie Night' has better mildew resistance than many, but is not unsusceptible. Plant it in good soil in sun and your plants will reach 90cm (36in).

SUNDIAL GARDEN

A successful garden is a space that reflects the personality and tastes of its owners and the people who use it every day, even when a designer has been brought in to design it. So when your clients are avid clock collectors, the natural choice is to form an outdoor sun clock to record the time of day as the sun moves through the sky from sunrise to sunset. Although this clock becomes the dominant feature within the space, with the clients' keen interest in gardening, the rest of the garden is not ignored. There is also a pond complete with fish and aquatic and marginal plants, mixed borders crammed with flowers, foliage and a scattering of vegetables, and a large deck from which to sit back and admire the view.

PLANNING the GARDEN

This garden was a corner plot attached to an urban end-of-terrace house, surrounded by a scattering of large shrubs, without houses directly overlooking it. Although close to the hustle and bustle of city life, the garden was quite private and reminiscent of the country. These factors gave me some freedom in the design as it did not have to adhere to the usual rule of being integrated with its urban landscape – and with all that privacy, we could have some fun.

It was decided to accentuate the country feel of the garden by keeping it as green as possible. A large lawn would anchor the space, with deep, generous beds around its perimeter allowing maximum planting opportunities. The owners, who were keen gardeners, wanted their garden not simply to be ornamental but also to embrace as diverse a range of plants as possible, combining productive vegetables with herbaceous perennials and plenty of shrubs.

Even in a limited space it is perfectly possible to mix mediums if you want to grow some of your own food. The beauty of vegetables is so often overlooked; their bright, attractive flowers could give some perennial blooms a run for their money and are followed by a plump, colourful crop. As the sight and smell of delicious, ripe courgettes, sweetcorn, tomatoes and runner beans is unsurpassed even before cooking, you could easily be fooled into believing you were in the country.

The owners' home was filled with a wealth of collected clocks, so we agreed that the garden should echo their passion by including a clock at its heart. Sundials have always been at home in the garden, watching the passage of time and marking the longest and shortest days of the year. It is

Natural light can supplemented with lanterns and nightlight holders, creating an easy understated glow when the sun goes down.

easy to see the attraction of sundials and they certainly have a long heritage. As early as 3500 BC the Egyptians began building slender obelisks, their moving shadows separating the day into sections measured with markers arranged around the base of the obelisk.

A circular base rising to a height of 45cm (18in) from ground level would become the clock face here. Raising it was not just for aesthetic reasons but also to make the clock easier to read. The 'dial' would be woven from willow to stress the country theme. Backfilled with soil and covered with turf, it would also double as a seating area.

So often when inheriting a garden, the terrace is a huge disappointment. Here, a thick concrete raft formed the seating area outside the rear of the house and would form a solid foundation for a deck that would simply clad the whole area. The front panels would be formed from woven willow, a great camouflage and a good tie-in to the woven willow sundial.

Near the terrace, in the existing garden layout, a water lily lay languishing in the tiniest of ponds, sharing its home with well over 60 fish. Both urgently needed some attention. It was decided that the pond should be moved to the bottom of the garden where it would not be so prominent, would look more naturally sited and would receive less direct sunlight. This was important because less light would generally promote the health of the pond for both plant and animal life.

Overall, I wanted to create a lasting design, sympathetic to the garden's unusually green urban surroundings, with a sundial as centrepiece to track the passing of the seasons and the plant life through its annual metamorphosis.

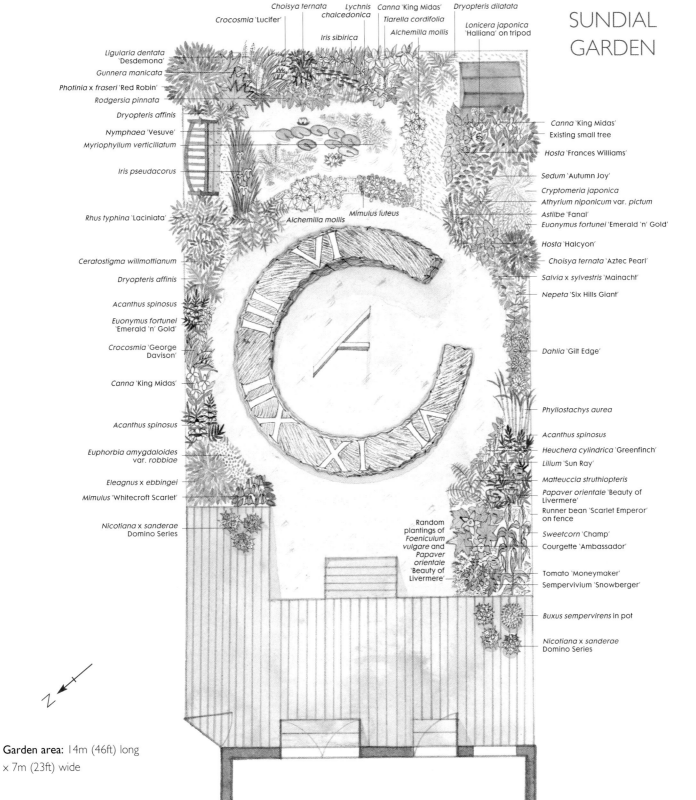

SUNDIAL
GARDEN

Choisya ternata
Crocosmia 'Lucifer'
Lychnis
chalcedonica
Canna 'King Midas'
Tiarella cordifolia
Alchemilla mollis
Dryopteris dilatata
Iris sibirica
Lonicera japonica
'Halliana' on tripod

Ligularia dentata
'Desdemona'
Gunnera manicata
Photinia x fraseri 'Red Robin'
Rodgersia pinnata
Dryopteris affinis
Nymphaea 'Vesuve'
Myriophyllum verticillatum
Iris pseudacorus

Rhus typhina 'Laciniata'

Alchemilla mollis
Mimulus luteus

Ceratostigma willmottianum
Dryopteris affinis

Acanthus spinosus
Euonymus fortunei
'Emerald 'n' Gold'
Crocosmia 'George
Davison'
Canna 'King Midas'

Acanthus spinosus

Euphorbia amygdaloides
var. robbiae
Eleagnus x ebbingei
Mimulus 'Whitecroft Scarlet'

Nicotiana x sanderae
Domino Series

Canna 'King Midas'
Existing small tree
Hosta 'Frances Williams'
Sedum 'Autumn Joy'
Cryptomeria japonica
Athyrium niponicum var. pictum
Astilbe 'Fanal'
Euonymus fortunei 'Emerald 'n' Gold'
Hosta 'Halcyon'
Choisya ternata 'Aztec Pearl'
Salvia x sylvestris 'Mainacht'
Nepeta 'Six Hills Giant'

Dahlia 'Gilt Edge'

Phyllostachys aurea
Acanthus spinosus
Heuchera cylindrica 'Greenfinch'
Lilium 'Sun Ray'
Matteuccia struthiopteris
Papaver orientale 'Beauty of
Livermere'
Runner bean 'Scarlet Emperor'
on fence
Sweetcorn 'Champ'
Courgette 'Ambassador'
Tomato 'Moneymaker'
Sempervivium 'Snowberger'
Buxus sempervirens in pot
Nicotiana x sanderae
Domino Series

Random
plantings of
Foeniculum
vulgare and
Papaver
orientale
'Beauty of
Livermere'

Garden area: 14m (46ft) long
x 7m (23ft) wide

SPECIAL FEATURES

Adeck formed the terrace directly outside the house, but this would not be the anchor that the terrace usually provides in a garden. Here, the centrepiece was to be the unusual sundial. Reflecting the owners' passion for clocks, it would provide an appropriate focal point – not just a timepiece but a conversation piece, too. The rest of the garden would emanate from the central raised dial of the sun clock.

Sundial

If you wanted to create a sundial in your own garden, the design opportunities are endless. There are several types of sundial to choose from, with complicated principles and techniques required in order to gauge the movements of the sun accurately. Although we engaged the services of an expert to help with the construction, our dial was based upon very simple principles using a long stout piece of timber to mark the time.

The earliest and simplest form of sundial is a shadow stick, or 'gnomon', which is still used by nomadic people as a method of timekeeping. The stick is positioned vertically and, as the sun moves through the sky from sunrise to sunset, the shadow of the gnomon rotates. It is shortest when the sun is in the south and at this point marks noon. However, because of the earth's tilt, the sun's path through the sky changes slightly every day. This of course means that the shadow of the gnomon varies slightly each day, too. Angling the gnomon and aiming it north overcomes this problem.

When a gnomon is angled in this way, it becomes known as a style.

Now tilted, the style's alignment compensates for the earth's tilt, so the hours marked by its shadow remain the same all year round (unless you live in the UK when the time changes by moving forward an hour from GMT in summer). Essentially, the method above was the one used in constructing our sundial.

Though our sundial was not 100 per cent accurate, the time only slips marginally, so once the time was set it would be accurate enough to be read all summer long. Wooden roman numerals

Grooved timber decking boards provide a good non-slip surface for wet or muddy shoes

Don't forget about the front facing edge of a deck. Leaving it open reveals the unattractive joists and cross braces that support the structure as a whole. Some kind of facing board, or as here a willow detail to tie in with the garden's signature feature, gives a polished finish that improves the overall design

Freestanding roman numerals were used to mark the numbers on our sundial – they can be moved to keep in line with the sun's time as it changes year on year, allow easy grass cutting and can be brought inside for winter protection

were ideal for marking the passage of time, and each piece could easily be moved each year to mark the changing passage of the sun, and of course for mowing the turf seat.

Clock face

The sundial face was to be circular in construction, in order to make it easier to read the time, but in design terms this sweeping arc also wrapped around the gnomon at the heart of the garden to provide a dramatic centrepoint. Willow was used as the main construction material for the dial. A supple material, willow is easily manipulated to form sweeping curves, so it was ideal for constructing the clock face. Rising from the ground to echo the rise of the sun at daybreak, the dial also doubled as a long bench from which the rest of the garden could be viewed and enjoyed.

Raised seat

A hollow, long 'box' was constructed from pliable, easily manipulated willow to act as the clock's dial and also function as a living bench. A frame was created by forcing thick hazel sticks into the ground, forming solid uprights for willow withies to be woven around, leaving a central void. This hollow centre was then lined with a weed-proof membrane to keep backfilled topsoil in position and to stop weeds from growing through the sides of the bench. A carpet of turf was laid on top of the soil, ultimately creating not just a clock face but also a natural seat of green.

Pond

The owners of this garden had already taken the plunge and added a pond. However, its occupants (fish and plants) had long outgrown it. The original pond was squeezed close to the house, where it looked very unnatural and as uncomfortable as surely its inhabitants must have been. More space was available at the rear of the garden, where in time plants would grow over the flexible liner that formed a new, larger informal wildlife pond. Once marked out, the pond was dug out (ensuring that the cavity was level), incorporating a 30 x 30cm (1 x 1ft) shelf around the edge to become home to marginal plants. Gently sloping sides to this shelf would allow wildlife to climb out easily and would stop the sides of the pond from crumbling. The central cavity was dug out next to a further depth of 60cm (2ft), and the whole area was lined with a protective layer of soft sand. A flexible butyl rubber liner was then draped over the whole cavity and weighted at the edges as the pool was filled with water. We siphoned water from the existing pool first in order to transport any existing pond life into the new pool and then the level was topped up. Finally, any excess liner was cut away. The new pond was then edged with pebbles and gravel.

With so much of the garden's area taken over by the central feature of the sundial, a large seating area was required from which to admire both it and the rest of the garden's elements. The previous owners had built a large concrete terrace immediately outside the house, long since past its best and now cracked and chipped with age and neglect. Though certainly not an aesthetically pleasing terrace, with its deep foundations it would provide the perfect base for underlying joists that would form the structural support for the boarded surface. A U-shaped deck emerged to reach into the garden and frame the willow sundial, with one arm of the U shape converted into a raised planting bed and the other formed into an extended seating area. The raised planting bed became a transitional area between the soft planting within the garden and the hard seating. This area was the obvious location for transitory annual plantings of vegetables or bedding plants, its character changing year on year.

As keen gardeners, it was important that the owners be able to use the garden throughout the year no matter the weather, so fluted decking boards laid crosswise to the direction in which

Above Once the designer has left, look around for interesting garden ornaments that will make the garden your own. This garden burner is attractive but functional, too …

Left … while this topiary frame adds a sense of fun to the space.

A garden pond complete with a good selection of fish and plants will become an ecosystem in its own right, inviting beneficial insects and wildlife into your garden.

people would be walking were screwed into position. Grooved decking planks provide a non-slip surface that wet and muddy shoes can easily grip, which is important if you are going to do any hard digging through the winter months. Laying boards crosswise to the direction you will be walking enhances their non-slip specification, and also creates a useful optical illusion in a small garden: with lines of boards reaching from left to right of the garden as opposed to front to back, the width of the garden is opened up to make a narrow area seem much wider than it truly is.

Generously proportioned steps into the garden made access easy and provided an impromptu, informal seating area. The whole area was finished off with a nod to the garden's centrepiece, the raised willow sundial. By fixing the deck's front with willow, a visual link was created, but this also provided a screen to conceal the deck supports and any of the original concrete terrace that would have otherwise shown through.

PLANTS and PLANTING

This was an unpretentious space where experimentation was to be encouraged; there was no time for designer-led plant snobbery here. It was a sunny space with good, free-draining loam, allowing for a wide range of plants. The problem was selecting just a few to fit into the limited area of ground.

Plants were chosen to form an eclectic, free-form mix. Annuals, herbaceous perennials, shrubs, aquatics, ferns and grasses would form an ever-changing space with myriad textures and forms for the owners, both keen gardeners, to enjoy. This was to be a garden for a gardener to flex his or her horticultural muscles. The planting was very much client-led, allowing them the space to add to the scheme in whatever way they wished.

Stately, handsome blooms, lilies come in several forms, with over 100 species to choose from. You cannot go wrong with *Lilium* 'Sun Ray' – not only beautiful but reliable, too.

Originating from the Americas and Australia, *Nicotiana* has a free-flowering nature over a long period in summer. *Nicotiana x sanderae* Domino Series are perfect half-hardy annuals for inclusion in the mixed border.

Lilium 'Sun Ray' (zones 3–8) is a strong grower. With a few exceptions, most lily bulbs are planted in autumn into well-dug soil with an addition of compost, drainage-improving sharp sand and a slow-release fertilizer. The genus *Lilium* is classified into nine divisions, and *L.* 'Sun Ray' is included in division 1a. This is the group of Asiatic Hybrids, plants derived from a group of mainly Asiatic lilies, giving rise to a very popular hardy range of lilies. Subdivided into three again – upright-flowered, outward-facing and pendant – *L.* 'Sun Ray' is an upright-flowering form. Blooming from early to midsummer and reaching a height of up to 1m (3ft), what this plant lacks in scent it makes up for in stature.

Nicotiana x *sanderae* Domino Series (zones 10–11) are ideal summer bedding annuals, opening their blooms proudly in full sun throughout the day. Simple flowers, their faces held upwards so they can be easily seen, bloom in a wonderful array of colours ranging from lime-green through delicate pink, red and purple, reaching an overall height of 45cm (18in). They are best raised from seed, so sow them in a propagator in early spring, pricking them out into deep seed trays or pots to grow on until they are ready to plant out into their final growing positions in early summer.

Long before runner beans are ready to harvest, the blooms look good enough to eat. Here, *Phaseolus coccineus* 'Scarlet Emperor' is mixed with cerise sweet peas, adding perfume to colour.

The sunny yellow flower and large leaves of *Cucurbita pepo* 'Ambassador' make this a valuable addition to the mixed border for the urban gardener, creating a visual not to mention edible feast.

There is nothing like the sweet juicy taste of tomatoes picked and eaten straight from the plant in late summer. *Lycopersicon* 'Moneymaker' is one of the most popular and reliable varieties.

Phaseolus coccineus **'Scarlet Emperor'** (all zones) is a traditional, early variety of runner bean, a reliable favourite that crops heavily and tastes as good today as it did when first introduced at the turn of the 1900s. Runner beans need a rich, well-dug, moisture-retentive soil in order to thrive and can be sown direct in late spring, or brought on earlier if sown in a greenhouse. Plant them alongside cane wigwams, up a fence or a netted frame about 20cm (8in) apart, and keep them well watered. Scarlet-red flowers will give rise to 25–30cm (10–12in) long pods. Harvesting will run from late summer into early autumn; regular picking will keep your plants producing crops.

Cucurbita pepo **'Ambassador'** (all zones) is one of a new breed of courgette that has been specifically bred to grow small fruits (courgettes are simply immature marrows, and in the past you had to sow marrow seed and pick the fruit before they became too large). Plants can take up a fair amount of space so grow your plants in containers if you really are strapped for space. Sow outdoors in late spring and keep your plants well watered as they grow, but do not sprinkle water directly on top of them. When the flowers give way to fruit, give them a weekly feed, picking the first fruits in summer when they are about 10cm (4in) long. Regular picking will encourage more fruit.

Lycopersicon **'Moneymaker'** (all zones) needs to grow in rich, moisture-retentive soil in a sunny, sheltered position. Set out your tomatoes 45cm (18in) apart in early summer, staking each one with a strong bamboo cane. Regularly remove side shoots from the leaf joints and pinch out the tops of the plants when four fruit trusses have formed. To maximize your crop, water them frequently and apply a liquid fertilizer once a week as the fruits start to develop. The tomatoes should be ready to pick in late summer. Leave the fruits on the plant until they are fully ripe.

Just as the garden begins to fade, dahlias produce strident, eye-catching colour, size and flower shapes in late summer and autumn. *Dahlia* 'Gilt Edge' is just one of some 20,000 cultivars.

Of all the shrubs, none is so versatile as *Buxus sempervirens*. Used for hedging, topiary, within borders, in containers and in knot gardens, evergreen boxwood is neverendingly useful.

Myriophyllum verticillatum may not be the most exciting plant to look at, but it is certainly the most attractive of a pond's indispensable oxygenating plants.

Dahlia **'Gilt Edge'** (zones 9–11) is a favourite of mine but you can choose from pom-pom, collerette, medium or giant cactus cultivars, small decorative or water lily. Their brazen blooms and long flowering season will soon endear dahlias to you. Plant the tubers in mid-spring in fertile, humus-rich soil, inserting stakes at planting time to secure the stems as they grow. Keep the tubers well watered, giving them a high-nitrogen fertilizer weekly in early summer, switching to a high-potash fertilizer each week from midsummer to early autumn. Dead-head the flowers as they fade, then in mid-autumn, after the first frost, lift the tubers carefully, allowing them to dry naturally before brushing them off and storing them over winter in a cool, dry, frost-free place. You can leave dahlias in the ground in relatively frost-free areas with a dry mulch.

Buxus sempervirens (zones 5–8), or box, tolerates any soil type, but the better the soil, the stronger and quicker the growth. It seems that you can throw almost any garden situation at box as this shrub endures full sun to deep shade, though variegated or golden-leaved forms may lose their colour given these conditions. Clip box three to four times during its growing season, beginning in spring when its fresh green growth begins to look unbearably messy. *B. sempervirens* is perfect for training into topiary shapes, while *B.s.* 'Suffruticosa' is better suited to edging paths and flowerbeds, its low, slow-growing nature cutting down on maintenance. The eventual height and spread of box ultimately depends upon you; at maturity box can reach a height and spread of 4 x 4m (13 x 13ft).

Myriophyllum verticillatum (zones 5–8), like the majority of oxygenating plants, is submerged, so it has little ornamental importance. However, it plays a vital functional role. Oxygenators absorb excess minerals from the water of the pond that, if left unchecked, would provide food for microscopic green algae that would quickly turn the pond water into thick green soup. They also convert carbon dioxide and absorb other waste products from fish. *M. verticillatum* (literally meaning 'many leaved') is best introduced into a pond by dropping weighted strands into the water in spring. The eventual height and spread of this plant varies depending upon the pond's characteristics and the species used.

Zea mays 'Champ' FI is extremely easy to grow. With its architectural foliage and loose feathery flowers, it is also a great decorative addition to the large mixed border.

Mixed varieties of sempervivum growing side-by-side create a stunning living collage. Here, *Sempervivum* 'Snowberger' is grown as a decorative edge to a border in open ground.

The water lily is the queen of the pond, indispensable for its beauty and for the shade of its leaves in maintaining a pond's delicate ecosystem. *Nymphaea* 'Vesuve' is suitable for most sizes of ponds.

Zea mays 'Champ' FI (all zones), or sweetcorn, will grow in almost any soil, requiring only a sunny, sheltered spot to do well. However, to grow quality cobs, dig some well-rotted manure or compost into the ground in the winter before planting, adding a general slow-release fertilizer (fish, blood and bone is ideal) just before you sow into the open ground. Late spring is the best time to sow direct, although you can sow seed earlier if it is given protection. Grow the plants in blocks rather than rows in order to ensure good pollination, water them well and in windy areas tie them to canes for support. The cobs will be ready to pick around six weeks after the silky tassels have appeared at the tops. When these tassels have started to go brown, check to see if cobs are ready by pulling back part of the sheath.

Sempervivum 'Snowberger' (zones 8–11) is a medium-sized houseleek, with soft grey-green rosettes, each with a faint reddish flush. It spreads quickly, covering 30cm (12in) effortlessly. It will grow almost anywhere if given full sun, even in the shallowest depth of soil. This allows for far-reaching planting opportunities – on shed roofs, in old piping, over bricks and even logs. If you choose to grow it in open ground, it requires a well-drained spot in full sun where it will not be covered or overhung by other plants. Give it a good mulch of gravel to protect its neck from the damp, and protect it from slugs; it will soon form a mass of rosettes. Flowers emerge on tall stems from the older rosettes in summer, and are reddish brown in colour.

Nymphaea 'Vesuve' (zones 4–9) is a hardy water lily developed by the French breeder Marliac during the 18th century. *N.* 'Vesuve' has a very long blooming season, and the flowers stay open longer than most, opening early in the morning and staying open until quite late in the day. When choosing a water lily it is important that you select the correct species for your pond. All water lilies have different growth rates, habits and leaf sizes. Read the label and check with your nursery before you buy the plant; an incorrect selection could lead to your water lily dominating the pond. *N.* 'Vesuve' is recommended for any size of water garden, except the smallest containers. Its flowers are produced above a floating raft of rounded leaves that cover the water's surface with a spread of up to 1.2m (4ft).

SECRET URBAN JUNGLE

Jungle, rainforest, beaches, sunshine, heat, hammocks, beers – just a few things that my clients missed on returning from a period working in New Zealand. I wanted to re-create a small part of New Zealand in their garden mixed with a sense of exploration and adventure. However, it was important that I did not overlook the new additions to the family: two young children under the age of five. The garden needed to be inviting for them, too, and safe for them to play in.

Added to these considerations was the garden's long, thin shape, so the design would not be straightforward. However, I had an advantage and a good start in the inherited mature planting at the garden's rear and boundary lines. It seemed obvious to me that, after a journey through the planting, the intrepid traveller should chance upon a resting place – an oasis of tranquillity away from the socializing area formed by a new raised terrace with seating outside the kitchen french windows.

PLANNING the GARDEN

It is unusual to find a small space that provides such different atmospheres from front to back; the back of this garden was divided from the front as if it had been split with a knife. Stepping from a sun-drenched terrace into overgrown undergrowth halfway down the space was like visiting a different continent. It was obvious why the garden appealed to my clients so much. Like those secret gardens of childhood, overgrown and romantic, this was a place for hiding away in dens – perfect for the young at heart.

Even though the overgrown sycamores, lilacs and even an oak in the surrounding gardens formed a fairly dense canopy, we could tackle what was on the ground within the garden to open up the space. Thinning out would allow enough light to enter the space to enable more manageable herbaceous plants to grow, with a few tropical accents thrown in for good measure. We were taking what many would think of as a disadvantage and turning it to our advantage by trying to work with the conditions, not against them. Plenty of organic matter dug into planting pits would help retain the moisture in the soil that so many tree roots were taking away, again allowing for a much wider variety of plants.

Changing levels and the use of specimen plants and shrubs to obscure various parts of the garden that lay behind added to a sense of mystery and helped increase the illusion of space within a relatively small plot.

With two young children, grass was a prerequisite for rough and tumble play, and also provided a formal grounding of green for the garden, shades of which were to form the basis of all the planting. Although the trees around the space were deciduous, leaving the garden bare in winter, many of

Nestled at the end of the garden, a gentle swing in your own hammock at the end of the day is the perfect way to escape from the stresses of the city.

the new plants were tropical, which on the whole meant evergreen. With a scattering of bulbs to take advantage of a canopy break in shade cover for a brief couple of months in spring, there would always be something to look at within the space, no matter the time of year. Smaller plants at ground level would shine through in winter and spring, and in summer would become overpowered by the rest of the scheme, with pinpoints of brightly coloured jungle blooms dominating visually.

As in any good, managed jungle, pathways would be constructed to guide visitors through the 'wilderness', with a bamboo grove rising centrally to obscure the way, thereby obliging the user to go round the canes to find what lay beyond: an easily constructed den for the children, and a clearing where the parents could chill out and escape from the mundanities of life.

From the house these two features would be barely visible, particularly as the decked terrace was to be raised above the main body of the garden, accessed via generous timber steps. Breaking up the space in this way and giving distinctly different features to the sections actually makes a space seem larger rather than smaller. Although you cannot see all the space in one viewing, this makes it more interesting; the two paths leading away from you are tantalizing – where do they lead? what might we find? In a garden with such a great emphasis on planting, and little apparent regard for ultimate heights and spreads, the whole effect seems otherworldly. Visitors loses their bearings, proportionally and visually, and you would not be surprised to see a parrot fly by or a monkey swing through the trees – all part of the original charm of the space, merely enhanced by the design.

SECRET URBAN JUNGLE

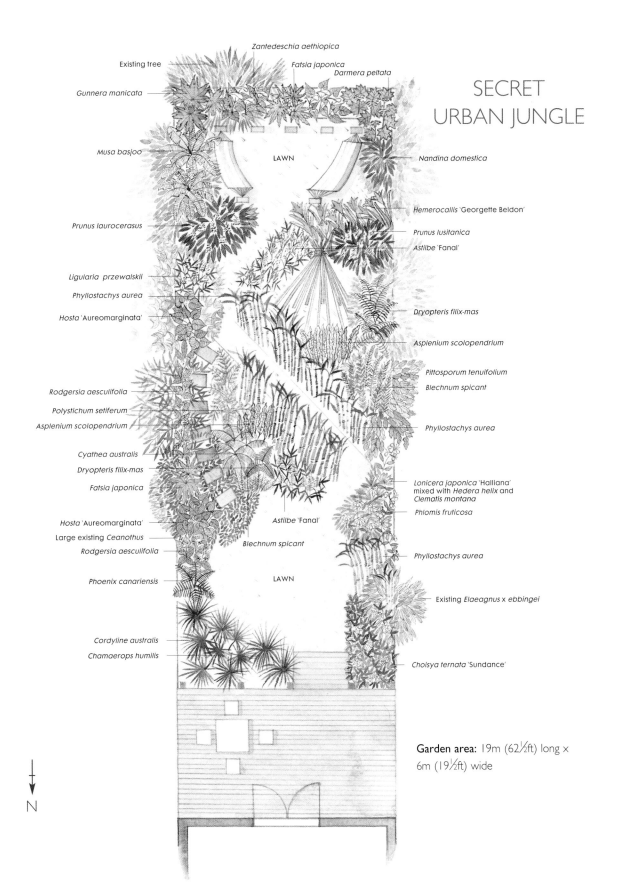

Existing tree

Zantedeschia aethiopica

Fatsia japonica

Darmera peltata

Gunnera manicata

Musa basjoo

LAWN

Nandina domestica

Hemerocallis 'Georgette Beldon'

Prunus laurocerasus

Prunus lusitanica

Astilbe 'Fanal'

Ligularia przewalskii

Phyllostachys aurea

Hosta 'Aureomarginata'

Dryopteris filix-mas

Asplenium scolopendrium

Pittosporum tenuifolium

Blechnum spicant

Rodgersia aesculifolia

Polystichum setiferum

Asplenium scolopendrium

Phyllostachys aurea

Cyathea australis

Dryopteris filix-mas

Fatsia japonica

Lonicera japonica 'Halliana'
mixed with Hedera helix and
Clematis montana

Phlomis fruticosa

Hosta 'Aureomarginata'

Large existing Ceanothus

Astilbe 'Fanal'

Rodgersia aesculifolia

Blechnum spicant

Phyllostachys aurea

Phoenix canariensis

LAWN

Existing Elaeagnus x ebbingei

Cordyline australis

Chamaerops humilis

Choisya ternata 'Sundance'

Garden area: 19m (62½ft) long ×
6m (19½ft) wide

N

SPECIAL FEATURES

In this garden the onus was to be upon plants rather than hard landscaping; greenery and blooms were to take centre stage. This would add to the jungle theme but was also because the budget available to redesign the garden was minimal. The majority of our funds were spent on resurfacing the ugly raised concrete patio outside the house. Cladding this in ribbed, pressure-treated softwood was the best, most achievable option. The concrete was solid enough to provide the perfect support for the decking framework of joists and lengths of timber that visually softened the area. Of course, not only is timber the best way to stretch a terracing budget, but it also saved us from going to the expense (and effort) of removing a huge raft of concrete.

Rope fencing

Where there is a raised terrace and younger children, some kind of support rail is essential. However, timber balustrade, steel wire supports or metal railings were prohibitively expensive. The ideal compromise was to use some kind of roping. This would also add interest to a large expanse of deck and link effortlessly into the tropical theme. Timber uprights were screwed home into the decking structure, and then pilot holes were drilled through the uprights themselves. This allows the rope to be threaded through the uprights, and knotted where necessary on each side of the uprights to keep it in position (this eliminates the danger of rope slipping through your fingers and burning you).

Rope absorbs moisture and shrinks as it becomes wet, so it is a good idea to wet the rope before fixing it so that it is pre-shrunk before you start. Remember that rope is essentially a plant material, so it will weaken and rot in time, potentially reaching a dangerous state in a few years. You could give it a coat of wood preservative to prolong its life but I think this looks unnatural; it is better to replace it before it becomes dangerous.

Right A frame of mature trees that completely enclose the garden at its boundaries allows complete privacy for pottering, play and relaxation away from the next door neighbours – essential no matter how nice they are.

Below Even a jungle garden needs a usable space for entertaining and eating al fresco. A low-key deck with rope fencing provides the perfect viewing platform from which to imagine your next garden adventure.

A quick, cheap and easy
garden den within a thicket
of bamboo encourages
imaginative play for young
children without costing a
fortune. Once outgrown,
the structure can simply
be removed and the area
reclaimed for more
exuberant planting.

Bamboo cane den

The lawn acts as the main play area in the garden, but I also wanted to include a space that would belong solely to the children. However, the children's needs would change as they grew, as would the parents' expectations of the garden, so I did not want to create anything that would be too permanent. Children do not need much in the way of structures in order to have fun in the garden – a blanket thrown over the limb of a tree will provide hours of fun. We wanted something that could be left out in all weathers and I decided that a simple bamboo structure would be ideal. Fifty canes, 2.5m (8ft) each in length, were pushed into the ground (this makes the whole structure stable and safe) in a circular shape and the tops were woven together and tied tightly with raffia (so much more attractive than ordinary string).

The children loved the structure. It provided them with a degree of privacy while allowing the parents to keep an eye on them through the open sides. When the children become bored with the den, it can be dismantled and the canes recycled as supports for the ever-growing plants.

Above Raffia blends with the bamboo canes as an informal tied brace for the play structure.

Below Always soak rope before incorporating it into fencing (or using as a support for roses) so that it is pre-shrunk.

Hammocks

For lying back, reading the Sunday papers, with a gin and tonic in hand while chatting over shared memories of travels abroad, what could be better than his and hers hammocks at the end of the garden. To my mind, no garden is complete without them. Supported by a railway sleeper at each end, the hammocks are held firmly in position, but the railway sleepers also have a sculptural quality. I extended the line of sleepers at the end of the garden to a total of five to provide a visual full stop and to echo the trees in the surrounding spaces without increasing the shade. Grouped like this, the sleepers were designed to be reminiscent of the tree trunks of huge specimen plants back in New Zealand.

Above When used vertically and concreted firmly into position, sleepers not only look great but also provide reliable support for hammocks. Look out for low-grade sleepers, which are cost effective and gnarled full of character.

Paths

There is no doubt that a garden's paths are its arteries, leading you around a space, revealing the garden's highlights and meandering away from its unsightly lows. The paths in this space were added in order to create movement and make the best use of the garden's overall floor space. Two paths were constructed. The first was a continuation of the lawn at the centre of the garden where a little light could get through an open canopy of shrubs (turf in too shady a spot can quickly become sludgy with regular use). The second path led right through the planting, a great coup for young children who are usually dissuaded from treading in such areas, making it easier to maintain plants at the heart of such a large planting bed. This planting path was created from reconstituted stone slabs to invite users, particularly children, to get up close and personal with the plants within the border. As the ferns in this area grow, it will become more and more secret, but the slabs will always provide not only a firm surface but also the invitation to walk through.

PLANTS and PLANTING

Planting a garden is without doubt one of the most enjoyable and satisfying processes for any garden designer. With thousands of plants to choose from, it is sometimes difficult to limit yourself to those few that will make the most of the space, particularly when a garden's size restricts your choice. In many ways it makes life easier to decide upon a themed planting style from the outset because this discipline will point you to plants that add to the theme, and the site and soil conditions will cut down the list of choices even further.

Writing a list of all the plants that will fit into the theme is the best way to start, choosing your accent specimens and then using a process of elimination for the rest. Cross out those plants that have requirements that do not fit with your own sun, shade or soil conditions, do not work with your developing colour scheme or do not work with the adjacent planting. Also consider ultimate height and spread, flowering season, texture and growth habit (or shape). This may seem like a lot to think about, but it is the fun part of the design process and, if you get it right, you will only need to update a strong theme with a few new additions from time to time.

Strong flower colour in shade is hard to come by, but provided the soil is damp, *Astilbe* 'Fanal' will perform at full pelt.

The leaves of *Rodgersia aesculifolia* are reminiscent of the horse chestnut tree – though when it comes to size, this plant is much more manageable.

Astilbe 'Fanal' (zones 4–9) produces dense panicles of crimson plumes in early summer that are longer lasting than those of most astilbe varieties, which only last up to around two weeks. They continue to look attractive even when past their best, contributing to the winter scene when encased in a layer of frost. These showy perennials grow well in moist borders, boggy watersides or in woodlands, and are admired not only for their blooms but also for their handsome froth of ferny foliage. Though a moist, humus-rich soil enables astilbes to grow in full sun, on drier soils a shadier spot is preferable; if the plant's fibrous roots dry out, the leaves dry to a crisp. A. 'Fanal' will ultimately reach a height of 60cm (24in).

Rodgersia aesculifolia (zones 5–9) enjoys much the same conditions as hostas but, unlike hostas, has huge, thick, leathery, corrugated, palm-shaped leaves. As a result, slugs and snails give this architectural plant a wide berth. Rodgersia varieties are blissfully tolerant of both acid and alkaline soil, and though they best enjoy moisture-retentive humus-rich soil in shade, they will grow in full sun provided they are poolside in a waterlogged soil. Drier areas are not a problem if they are in shade. Although their foliage makes them seem eminently jungle-worthy, their flowers also have a jurassic look to them, with panicles of creamy white to gently pink flowers rising in summer from the foliage to heights of about 1.8m (6ft), given the right conditions.

Each individual bloom of *Hemerocallis* 'Georgette Beldon' may be transient, but they are produced in such quick succession that you might not notice.

Gunnera manicata is the ultimate in prehistoric-looking plants; no jungle garden scheme would be complete without one.

An impressive vertical accent for the wilder garden, *Ligularia przewalskii* grows best in boggy, wet soil.

Hemerocallis 'Georgette Beldon' (zones 4–10) has scented dark pink, almost maroon-stained petals with a golden throat, but with over 30,000 named cultivars of this species available, you can mix and match to your heart's content. There is an amazing array of colours, flower sizes and shapes to choose from, so no matter what your scheme there is bound to be a variety for you. Easy to grow and tough to boot, this group of plants is equally accessible to seasoned plant collectors and novice gardeners alike. They look great when planted in drifts through a large border or in a wild garden, preferring fertile, moist, well-drained soil, but they are not too fussy and will happily bloom for a long season throughout the summer, reaching a height of around 80cm (32in).

Gunnera manicata (zones 6–10) is a huge herbaceous perennial, preferring deep, permanently moist soil in shade. However, it is perhaps best not to fulfill all its needs or it may take over your entire urban backyard. In ideal conditions, each leaf will reach a span of over 2m (6ft), held aloft on spiny stems that are themselves 2.5m (8ft) long. In colder, more exposed areas, the plant that is commonly known as poor man's umbrella (perfect shelter for anyone during a tropical downpour in its native Brazil) will need some winter protection. In autumn, cut and then fold its leaves over the crown, pinning them down carefully if required, and protect the crown for the winter with an additional layer of straw if necessary.

Ligularia przewalskii (zones 4–9) is a dream plant for many gardeners and, though it is not always readily available, it is well worth seeking out. The leaves are deeply divided, which, given their desirability to slugs and snails, is a very good thing; slug damage is more difficult to notice. In midsummer it produces elegant spikes of spidery bright yellow flowers held upon very dark slender stems. Ensure that the ground in which *L. przewalskii* is grown is deep and fertile, that plants are planted in direct sun (perhaps with some midday shade, as very hot weather leads to wilting), and you will encourage seeding. This graceful but rugged plant may even naturalize by seed given the right conditions, reaching an ultimate height of 2m (6ft).

The most commonplace shrubs often prove perfect for the urban gardener who is challenged for time. Here, *Choisya ternata* 'Sundance' edges the jungle garden perfectly.

In a jungle scheme there are some plants that you just cannot do without. Whether planted in a border or placed centre stage upon a terrace in its own pot, *Phoenix canariensis* adds drama to a garden.

With its large felty leaves and unusual attractive blooms, *Phlomis fruticosa* looks at home in any garden scheme – jungle, country or formal.

Choisya ternata **'Sundance'** (zones 7–10), or Mexican orange blossom as it is commonly known, is a reliable evergreen shrub that flowers in late spring through to early summer. The tiny white blooms, which it bears profusely, are slightly scented. *C.t.* 'Sundance' forms a useful rounded shape, adding structure even in the depths of winter, and looks good within a border as an accent plant or in groups spaced 80cm (32in) apart to form an informal hedge. Plant it in well-drained soil in full sun or light shade, but be aware that this plant does have a reputation for outgrowing its situation. To keep it in check, encourage flowering and to keep the foliage shiny, cut all the stems to 50cm (20in) every 3–4 years. Left unchecked its ultimate height and spread is 2.5 × 2.5m (8 × 8ft).

Phoenix canariensis (zones 8–10), or the Canary Island date palm, has to be one of the easiest palms to grow. If it is planted in fertile well-drained soil in full sun (though it does not object to a modicum of light shade), this vase-shaped mass of spiky leaves will quickly develop a trunk. When mature, the tightly grouped branches of foliage will spread to form broadly arching leaves reaching a staggering 4–6m (12–20ft) in length. If you have ambitions to grow a plant of this stature, be aware that it is frost-tender and will require winter protection; bring it into the greenhouse if it is portable or provide it with a good wrapping of horticultural fleece through the winter freeze. If you are lucky, this plant can reach an ultimate height of 15m (50ft), though this is unusual in all but the most tropical weather conditions.

Phlomis fruticosa (zones 8–10), or Jerusalem sage as it is commonly known, forms a rounded low ball of fuzzy leaves in felty grey, each leaf covered in a tactile soft down. Early to midsummer sees the shrub bring forth unusual whorled blooms of golden yellow, each flower bizarrely supporting others at their centre. For the very best results, give this plant lots of sun and dry, open soil; it detests any kind of waterlogging. Do be advised that it is wise to take cuttings of these plants as they are only borderline hardy; you may lose them in a particularly cold winter. Its ultimate height and spread at maturity is 1 × 1.2m (3 × 4ft).

A contentious plant (you either love ivy or hate it), there is no denying that, when used as a climber, *Hedera helix* provides a solid evergreen backdrop in the garden against which other plants can perform.

In its juvenile form, *Cordyline australis* is the perfect punctuation for the centre of a jungle border, its upright foliage providing an eye-catching and dramatic display while also suggesting movement.

A wonderfully enthusiastic plant that heralds the point when late spring becomes summer, *Clematis montana* is a fun, exuberant, vigorous early climber.

Hedera helix (zones 4–9) is an immensely useful plant, growing in almost any soil and in sun through to extremely deep shade. It will even grow in the worst of city pollution. It can be trained to grow up or drape down over walls or to carpet the ground. Although it has aerial roots, these are shallow enough not to damage the brickwork of a house if the brickwork is in good condition in the first place. Here, mid-green common or English ivy is grown along a fence to form a self-clinging understated backdrop to the plants and structures within the space. However, ivies are available in a wide range of colours, textures and leaf sizes. Mix several varieties together to form a tapestry of foliage to cover a large expanse of wall all year round. Its ultimate height and spread is 10 × 10m (33 × 33ft).

Cordyline australis (zones 9–11) has a clutch of sword-like leaves in light to almost yellow-green, each reaching up to 1m (3ft) in length. The cabbage palm is often planted as an accent plant, but bear in mind that the squat short stem that the plant produces will develop into a trunk as the plant grows into a tree reaching up to 10m (33ft) in height. Cordylines prefer well-drained dry soil in sun, and though they will fight off a degree of winter cold, they will only tolerate cold down to a temperature of -5°C (23°F). If you live in a cold climate, you are best advised to protect your plants under glass in winter. For best results through the summer, water your plants infrequently and apply a balanced liquid fertilizer once a month.

Clematis montana (zones 4–9) produces masses of vanilla-scented white and pink-blushed blooms for around four weeks in late spring, against a backdrop of dark green attractive leaves. Yellow anthers at the centre of each flat bloom make the flowers stand out even more against the foliage, creating a spectacular display that is hard to beat. Perfect for growing over sheds and summer houses, or to clothe large expanses of fence, *C. montana* is best planted in autumn or spring in good, fertile soil in a sunny spot. Simply ensure that you give this climber room to run as it will reach 14m (46ft) in height if allowed. *C. montana* flowers on the previous year's growth, so if you need to prune it back to keep it under control, do this as soon as flowering has finished or it will not bloom the following year.

MEDITERRANEAN HAVEN

Evenings spent lounging upon a terracotta terrace, scent dripping from the warm air, bees buzzing drunkenly through a jumble of bursting bloom … it is no wonder that the Mediterranean garden is so well loved. This south-facing garden, soaked in sunshine for most of the day, would accommodate a Mediterranean look perfectly. Free from her old lawn, the owner could relax and potter among containers and borders filled with the scent of aromatics, and be transported to sunnier climes after a hard day's work.

PLANNING the GARDEN

A keen gardener but with a full-time job, the owner of this space was tired of struggling with a high-maintenance lawn. With precious little free time, she wanted to relax and do only those gardening jobs she enjoyed. It was decided that the time-consuming grass lawn was to be removed and be replaced with more suitable low-maintenance surfacing materials.

Plants were to take centre stage, and with such an abundance of sun it was important to get the planting right. There is much to be said for the adage 'right plant, right place'. Fighting against your space will always provide some casualties of battle, and will also wear you out in the end. This south-facing plot received strong summer sun throughout the day, so it was decided to use a majority of plants originating from the Mediterranean. Plants that thrive in strong sunlight in poor soils would certainly enjoy the conditions here. A gravel surface to the garden would provide a mulch to keep out weeds and to protect the plants against frost, also keeping plant growth from direct contact with the soil that in wet conditions could potentially lead to rot. Planting into gravel in this way provides a low-key, natural-looking informality that many people adore. Gravel not only looks good in its own right as it meanders through a space, filling any tight corners or awkward spaces, but is also a good bridging material, linking areas together. Mixed with planting, gravel locks shifting plant shapes, textures, heights and colours together to form a harmonious whole. I used it as a mulch on the main body of planting around the boundaries of the garden, easing it out

Choose garden accessories that blend in with the colours of your planting scheme. Here, an old favourite, blue and yellow, has a laidback, sunny Mediterranean vibe.

centrally to form an underfoot surface with a random scattering of plants. This random planting forms a style of 'escapee' planting that pre-empts the self-seeding that will undoubtedly occur as plants find their own way.

A Mediterranean-influenced garden would not be complete without a terracotta terrace on which to entertain friends and family for long al fresco dinner parties during balmy summer evenings. Terracotta tiles, like brick, are formed from clay but are dried in the sun. Mottled, mellow tones in the terracotta's surface awaken one's memories of lazy days spent in sunnier climes, thereby underlining the atmosphere I was striving to create.

However, there is no denying that sun-baked spots can be too much for some people and a cooler, shadier area is often a welcome respite from the heat of the sun on very hot days. A secondary terrace at the end of the garden would not only provide another focus but also a modicum of shade and shelter.

Finally, a small water feature would add to the sensory pull of the space, contributing another cooling element to the garden as well as the ever-desirable sound of rippling water.

The plants would be the icing on the cake, the ultimate styling ingredient, chosen either because they originate from the Mediterranean or because they enjoy similarly hot, harsh conditions. Aromatics with contrasting textures and shapes spilling into one another would form an understated wild look and release their hidden asset of scent as visitors brush past them.

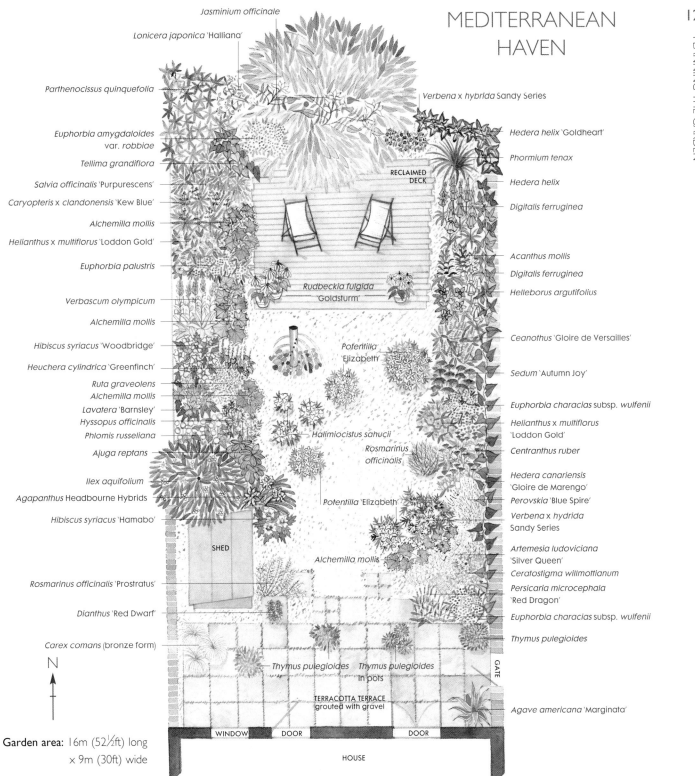

Jasminium officinale

Lonicera japonica 'Halliana'

Parthenocissus quinquefolia

Verbena x hybrida Sandy Series

Euphorbia amygdaloides
var. robbiae

Hedera helix 'Goldheart'

Tellima grandiflora

Phormium tenax

Salvia officinalis 'Purpurescens'

Hedera helix

Caryopteris x clandonensis 'Kew Blue'

Digitalis ferruginea

Alchemilla mollis

Helianthus x multiflorus 'Loddon Gold'

RECLAIMED
DECK

Euphorbia palustris

Acanthus mollis

Digitalis ferruginea

Helleborus argutifolius

Verbascum olympicum

Rudbeckia fulgida
'Goldsturm'

Alchemilla mollis

Hibiscus syriacus 'Woodbridge'

Ceanothus 'Gloire de Versailles'

Heuchera cylindrica 'Greenfinch'

Potentilla
'Elizabeth'

Sedum 'Autumn Joy'

Ruta graveolens

Alchemilla mollis

Euphorbia characias subsp. wulfenii

Lavatera 'Barnsley'

Helianthus x multiflorus
'Loddon Gold'

Hyssopus officinalis

Halimiocistus sahucii

Phlomis russeliana

Centranthus ruber

Ajuga reptans

Rosmarinus
officinalis

Ilex aquifolium

Hedera canariensis
'Gloire de Marengo'

Agapanthus Headbourne Hybrids

Potentilla 'Elizabeth'

Perovskia 'Blue Spire'

Verbena x hybrida
Sandy Series

Hibiscus syriacus 'Hamabo'

Artemesia ludoviciana
'Silver Queen'

SHED

Alchemilla mollis

Ceratostigma willmottianum

Persicaria microcephala
'Red Dragon'

Rosmarinus officinalis 'Prostratus'

Euphorbia characias subsp. wulfenii

Dianthus 'Red Dwarf'

Thymus pulegioides

Carex comans (bronze form)

GATE

N

Thymus pulegioides
in pots

Thymus pulegioides

Agave americana 'Marginata'

TERRACOTTA TERRACE
grouted with gravel

Garden area: 16m (52½ft) long
x 9m (30ft) wide

WINDOW   DOOR   DOOR

HOUSE

SPECIAL FEATURES

With its natural materials in understated tones, the hard landscaping emphasized the overall look without dominating the space. Instead its role was to act as a frame within which the wide range of deliciously aromatic and scented plants were crammed.

Terracotta and gravel surface

The easy-on-the-eye good looks of terracotta are perfect for this garden setting but, if you are planning to use terracotta, do check that the slabs are suitable for exterior use. If you fail to do so, you take the risk of an expensive investment cracking in low temperatures. Real terracotta can also be prohibitively expensive (though there is nothing quite like the real thing), but there are a wide range of extremely good imitations on the market, offering considerable cost savings. Always see a sample both dry and wet before you make your final selection.

Mixing tile sizes makes for a more authentic Mediterranean look. Though the design of this terrace began with a uniform pattern, this gradually gave way to larger spaces left between slabs until they were laid entirely randomly. Instead of grouting between the tiles, gravel was brushed into the gaps to add to the informal style. Gravel became the unifying feature of the garden, linking paving, planting and water feature together.

Reclaimed deck

Though small, the garden was large enough to incorporate a secondary terrace at the end of the space. This attractive seating area would invite users out into the garden, to pass through the intoxicating perfumes released by the surrounding plants. In order to create a feeling of instant age, I used reclaimed timber. Notched, stained and worn, lacking the uniformity of size and thickness of newly cut boards, and varying in colour and tone, timber is the most exciting of reclaimed materials for garden building. Here, it had the advantage of giving the garden a feeling of lived-in maturity the instant it was laid in position.

Reclaimed hardwood previously used as the floor of a pier was coaxed into forming the deck, requiring an investment in both time and patience. These hardworking planks are cantankerous old characters; new wood is far more eager and willing to be worked into shape. Here, the decking boards were held in position with a particularly solid frame, each hardwood board requiring pre-drilling before it was fixed into place.

Left The dynamic whirling motion of this steel water feature is emphasized by a spiralling curve of silver resin-coated gravel chippings scattered on top of the surrounding gravel surface.

Fences

Often there is not the budget to replace the fence of a garden when it is redesigned, and yet
fences are perhaps one of the most prominent features to leap out at you when a garden is
finished. I would urge anyone keen to give their garden a new look to consider the fences
surrounding their space. Here, two tones of a lilac paint were watered down and washed
over fence panels to create a feeling of age under the restrictions of a limited budget. With
very little investment in either time or money, a uniform tone and colour linked the varying
fence styles together to form an effective backdrop to the garden, its features and its plants.

Buzzing with colour, scent and wildlife, Mediterranean gardens look magnificent all summer long and by their natures are extremely low maintenance. This garden would require little in the way of watering or feeding, and with an expanse of gravel as the primary surfacing material and mulch, weeding is kept to a minimum. I included as many native Mediterranean plants (including rosemary, lavender and thyme) as possible, then sprinkled in those that enjoy the same conditions and would add contrast to the foliage, texture, shape and form of the scheme.

Using those plants in your garden that would happily grow in similar soil conditions in their native habitat creates a healthy, harmonious scheme requiring little in the way of assistance from you. The plants in this garden have an inherent affinity with each other because they would naturally grow together.

Euphorbia characias subsp. *wulfenii* gives structure to a garden, and its blue-green stems form an evergreen clump of year-round handsome foliage.

With its long flowering season, *Potentilla fruticosa* 'Elizabeth' earns its keep in the sunny gravel garden.

Euphorbia characias subsp. *wulfenii* (zones 8–10) sets the scene in the Mediterranean garden. Originating from this part of the world, its leathery upright stems are constant throughout the year, but it is not valuable for its structural presence alone. Early spring sees stems give rise to yellow-green bracts of unusual flowers, the perfect accompaniment to spring-flowering bulbs. To keep the foliage looking fresh, cut back stems that flowered earlier in the year to ground level in midsummer to force a fresh foliage display in autumn. Wear gloves while undertaking any kind of pruning of euphorbias; the milky sap that cut stems exude is a powerful skin irritant. This wonderful plant will reach an ultimate height and spread of 1.2 x 1.2m (4 x 4ft).

Potentilla fructosa 'Elizabeth' (zone 3–7) has grey-green foliage that is smothered in canary yellow flowers for months throughout the summer. Whether grouped in a mixed border, planted singly in a gravel garden or spaced about 60cm (2ft) apart to form a low informal hedge, this plant performs well in a very wide range of soils. It will grow almost anywhere, only becoming stressed in very wet, exceedingly dry or very alkaline conditions. Keep your plants productive by pruning back around one-third of their growth each year after flowering. Old plants can be hard pruned to the ground in spring if they have become straggly and will quickly reclaim their former glory. Its eventual height and spread is 1.2 x 1.2m (4 x 4ft).

A useful summer-flowering sub-shrub for the back of the border or centre stage in a large gravel garden, *Lavatera* 'Barnsley' flowers continuously throughout the summer.

Persicaria microcephala 'Red Dragon' adds drama and exotic interest to the garden. Pointed metallic grey leaves, each marked with a plum chevron at the centre, are set against red stems.

A hot, dry summer is required to enable you to enjoy the sumptuous blooms of *Hibiscus syriacus* 'Woodbridge'.

Lavatera 'Barnsley' (zones 6–9) has a very long blooming period with large flowers, each up to 7cm (3in) across, and with an overall height and spread of 2 x 2m (6 x 6ft) – no wonder it is such a favourite. Each flower is formed of deeply notched petals of white that fades to soft pale pink with age. In areas prone to severe frost, grow the plant against a sunny sheltered wall out of the reach of cold, drying winds. *L.* 'Barnsley' grows best in full sun on light, moderately fertile, well-drained soil. A short-lived plant, it is advisable to take softwood cuttings in early summer, propagating regularly to ensure replacement plants if required. *L.* 'Barnsley' benefits from a hard prune almost to ground level in spring and pinching the stems back hard in early summer.

Persicaria microcephala 'Red Dragon' (zones 4–9) is a vigorous grower but is not invasive, happily mixing with other perennials without overpowering them. Its ultimate height is 60cm (24in), with a slightly larger spread of 80–100cm (30–40in). Enjoying both sun and light shade, though flamboyant this plant is no prima donna, tolerating most soil types, even heavy clay. Small white flowers are produced in early summer, but these are insignificant and certainly secondary to the plant's amazing foliage.

Hibiscus syriacus 'Woodbridge' (zones 5–8) is a half-hardy shrub that tolerates temperatures down to -15°C (4°F), so do not be too hasty in your assessment of it in spring. Leaf formation in hibiscus can be very late, leading you to think that your shrub has not survived the winter. Though some flowering shrubs may be damaged by late frosts, if grown in a sheltered position in the garden, your plant may well have survived; move your plants into the greenhouse before the first frost if you are unwilling to take the risk. Large, open blooms in rich deep pink, each petal with a dark pink splotch at its centre, make this plush, lavish plant appear deeply exotic. Its eventual height and spread is 3 x 2m (10 x 6ft).

Grasses like *Carex comans* (bronze form) are endlessly useful in the garden, their lax, graceful habit adding texture to the border or creating a statement in a pot.

Ajuga reptans 'Catlin's Giant' is semi-evergreen and can make an unusual container plant, its young dripping from the parent plant down the container's sides.

Dianthus 'Red Dwarf' provides excellent scarlet colour in mid- to late summer, and is at home in a wide variety of situations including the rock garden, scree plantings, at the front of borders and in pots.

Carex comans (bronze form) (zones 4–8) can be grown in full sun to light shade, its graceful habit and bronzed tones providing the perfect accompaniment to gravel, no matter where you choose to site it. Here on the terracotta terrace, it softens the lines of hard landscaping while complementing the hue of the clay tiles. Reaching an overall height of 30cm (12in) and spread of 75cm (30in), these tussock grasses originate from New Zealand where they can be seen spectacularly covering whole hillsides. They will grow in a wide variety of soils apart from those with extremes of wet or dry.

Ajuga reptans 'Catlin's Giant' (zones 4–8) is a large-leaved variety whose stained pewter-bronze leaves create considerable impact. Each leaf can reach up to 15cm (6in) in length and the late spring blue flower-spikes are larger than the parent variety's too, hitting 20cm (8in) in height. It will tolerate any quality of soil, even very impoverished ground. No matter where you plant it, creeping rhizomes will spread quickly to colonize an area. Overall the plant can reach roughly 45cm (18in) in height, but will spread to around 1m (3ft).

Dianthus 'Red Dwarf' (zones 4–8) is a plant I like to grow in a container to raise its comparatively large flowers away from the ground so that their scent can be enjoyed more easily. There is an added advantage to this in that dwarf pinks enjoy the sharp drainage so easily provided within a container. *D.* 'Red Dwarf' requires little maintenance, though it is a good idea to snip off spent flower-heads to maintain healthy plants. The ultimate height of this dianthus is 10cm (4in) and the spread is 20cm (8in).

No Mediterranean planting scheme would be complete without thyme. *Thymus pulegioides* planted in a small pot can be moved at whim so that you can always enjoy the scent released from its leaves.

A highly evocative plant, *Agave americana* 'Marginata' instantly sweeps you away to sunnier climes and is happy in a gravel bed or in a container.

Neat and compact, annual verbenas offer summer impact in a wide range of colours. *Verbena x hybrida* Sandy Series give a long-lasting, vivid performance.

Thymus pulegioides (zone 5–9) is a spreading sub-shrub that also lends itself to crevice planting, useful for enlivening a tired terrace or pathway. Each time it is brushed past or stepped upon it releases an intoxicating perfume. Thyme needs well-drained soil in full sun in order to thrive. Late spring and early summer see short spikes of pinky purple flowers that are soon engulfed by the lazy buzz of bees – the perfect accompaniment to an evening glass of sangria. Your plants will reach a height of 5–25cm (2–10in), depending on their site and cultivation method. Remember to cut the blooms back when they have finished flowering to keep your plants compact.

Agave americana 'Marginata' (zones 8–11) is a ferocious beauty with spined tips and leaf margins (give this plant a wide berth and consider excluding it altogether if you have young children). Originating from Mexico, it is not completely hardy and may need winter protection, though larger specimens in warmer areas may survive a mild winter. If grown in a pot, the plant can quickly be whisked into a greenhouse when autumn frosts arrive. The other advantage of container-grown plants is that they will regularly produce offspring from the base that can easily be removed, potted on and given away as gifts to friends. Its eventual height and spread is 2 x 3m (6 x 10ft), though this size is reduced when grown in a pot.

Verbena x hybrida Sandy Series (zones 7–10) produce upright plants reaching a height of 25–30cm (10–12in) in a range of colours from rose pink and magenta to scarlet. Plants and seeds are usually sold in a mixed colour range, so you might have to take your chances on colour arrangement. Their small size makes them a perfect choice for growing in containers, hanging baskets and window boxes; a low bowl arranged as an outdoor centrepiece will enable you to enjoy the flowers close up. Be aware that it is susceptible to mildew, so make sure your plants are not allowed to dry out.

Every garden is unique, and your gardening experience will vary from region to region, governed by your garden's position, your local climate and variable weather conditions. Although your garden's position and soil type are constant, the weather can vary radically from year to year, making seasonal forecasting a hit-and-miss process. That is why gardening guides, while exceedingly helpful in ensuring that you do not forget to carry out a job, should be treated as just that: a guide. Ultimately, the decision whether to carry out a certain job at a particular time is down to you, should the time (and weather report) seem right.

SPRING

As spring jaunts merrily into our gardens, with its longer days, warmer weather and sunshine, it breathes a new lease of life into gardeners, too. However, before you leap into action too hastily, remember that spring is the most changeable of all the seasons; one minute it is sunny and bright, the next raining and cold. Try not to rush too enthusiastically into planting, pruning or splitting anything that might quickly be damaged by a sudden and unexpected frost.

Be prepared for some hard work. Spring cleaning your garden now will allow you to reap the rewards later in the year. This is one of the busiest times in the garden, so make sure you do not miss a trick.

Split your garden into different areas and deal with one section at a time. You could even photocopy the lists that follow and tick off each task as you complete it, and while you complete your list of chores, your garden will obligingly spring into life once more before your eyes.

SOIL TYPES | Understand your ground

There is no doubt that good, healthy soil leads to good, healthy plants. There are several types of soil, however, so it is a good idea to find out which category yours fall into before you plant anything. Soil type often dictates the kind of plants you will be able to grow, so check plant labels before purchase.

It might be obvious to you that yours is not the best soil in the world, but do not worry – soil type can be improved with an investment of time and effort. Waterlogged ground can be improved with the addition of drainage material, while sandy soil can be improved by adding compost and manure to force it to hold water more effectively.

The ideal soil is dark and crumbly, and full of earthworms. It is not too wet or too dry, and it usually takes work to achieve. When you do, you will find that this type of soil can support a huge range of plants.

Clay This is easy to identify: your ground will be heavy, difficult to dig, waterlogged and possibly smelly. Clay is cold and slow to warm up in spring. It is slippery and slimy when wet and sets rock hard after a dry summer spell. Roll a handful of soil about in your hands; if you can form it into a cigar shape and it holds the shape when you open your hand, you have clay soil. On the plus side, clay is extremely fertile and can be improved by digging it over in autumn and spring, adding well-rotted manure (fresh manure gives off ammonia as it rots, which is harmful to plants and uses up valuable nitrogen in the soil during its decomposition process), compost or lime in order to get the soil to crumble. Coarse sand or gravel will also help to open up the soil and make it easier to drain.

Sand is light, free draining and very crumbly. Water vanishes through it almost immediately, taking with it valuable nutrients, so feeding and watering are needed regularly. It warms up quickly in spring and is very easy to work with. This 'hungry' soil is easily improved with the addition of lots of compost or well-rotted manure (known as 'organic matter'); these particles act as miniature sponges, improving the ground's water- and nutrient-holding capabilities.

Silt is halfway between sand and clay in texture, but retains water in the same way (though not to the same degree) as clay. When wet, silt compacts down to form a hard layer, or 'pan', that plants have to struggle to grow down into.

Chalk is usually a very shallow soil that is free draining and alkaline; because water drains away from it relatively easily, it only has moderate fertility. It is very light in colour and often has actual lumps of chalk in it, making it easy to identify. Adding organic matter is the best way to improve a chalky soil, but as organic matter tends to decompose quickly in alkaline soils, it needs topping up regularly.

Acid or alkaline?

If it is not perfectly obvious what pH your soil is (that is, whether it is acid or alkaline) by taking a quick look over your neighbours' fences and seeing what type of plants are thriving in their gardens, it is a good idea to test it with a cheap testing kit available from all garden centres. Measuring the pH of your garden will be a good indicator as to which plants will, and more importantly will not, grow in your garden.

The pH of your garden will be within a scale ranging from 1 to 14. A pH below 7 indicates that you have an acid soil, ideal for acid-loving plants such as rhododendrons, azaleas and camellias, while a pH above 7 indicates an alkaline soil, a typically dry, well-draining soil that suits a wide range of perennials such as eryngium, verbascum, and pulsatilla. Neutral soil has a pH of 7 in which a wide range of plants will be happy.

Making compost

With so much importance placed on soil improvement, it is madness not to make your own compost. If you add kitchen and garden waste to a compost heap, about a year later you will get rich, crumbly soil. Buy a compost bin or make your own with some stout stakes supporting a chicken wire pen and then start piling the waste up. Once you have the bin, garden compost is completely free.

Besides grass clippings, all your garden waste can be added to the heap, although small branches should be chipped before they are included. Annual weeds (chickweed, groundsel and nettles) can be added without worry, provided they are not smothered in seed, but perennial weeds should only be added at the centre of a very 'hot' compost heap. Lots of kitchen waste can be incorporated, provided it has not been cooked; fruit, vegetables, teabags, eggshells and coffee grindings are all ideal. Do not add bones, meat or fat because these will attract rats. Paper, cardboard and egg boxes can be added but must be well shredded first.

Make sure you mix up the layers, adding lots of dry material (such as dry leaves, dry grass and straw) to the heap and turning the whole thing at least once. Both will add air, which is essential to the decomposition process. This process will generate heat and speed up decomposition. In the small urban garden, where a homemade compost bin may not be large enough to produce enough heat, an insulated manufactured composter is the best way to encourage it decomposition.

Finally, an activator will also speed things up. Sulphate of ammonia, nettles and even urine are all good activators.

Wormeries are ready-made bins suitable for the small urban garden; a colony of worms breaks down kitchen waste in an extremely clean, efficient process. In fact, the process is so tidy that you can even keep the bin in your kitchen.

Trees and shrubs

- While trees and shrubs are still dormant, complete any new plantings into open ground or containers, weather permitting.
- Feed established shrubs with a slow-release fertilizer that will nourish them throughout the coming summer.
- In early spring cut out any dead, damaged or diseased wood from trees and shrubs to maintain their health and vigour.
- Coppice and pollard trees in early to mid-spring.
- Check and adjust tree stakes and their supporting ties.
- In late spring, deadhead any winter-flowering shrubs you are not collecting seed from.
- Prune winter and early flowering shrubs in late spring when they have finished blooming, shrubs that flower on new wood and all hydrangeas.
- Cut the previous year's stems of *Salix* and *Cornus* grown for winter colour back to

Routine jobs for spring

- Apply a slow-release fertilizer to trees, shrubs, border, fruit and perennial vegetables to release nutrients to plants throughout the coming summer.

- Wage war on the weeds that steal nutrients, water, light and space from cultivated plants.

- Mulch flowerbeds once they are moist and weed-free.

- Dig over new borders to break up the soil for planting.

- Keep a look out for slugs and snails and remove any you see immediately; empty upturned grapefruit halves, beer traps and nematodes are other organic controls you could use.

- Begin weeding any gravel paths before the seedlings begin to flower, which will result in more offspring to dispose of.

- Hoe off any weeds you see within the borders as soon as they appear.

ground level. This will ensure you will also have a good display the following winter.
- Take softwood cuttings in mid- to late spring.
- Give topiary its first trim.
- Remove suckers rising from the roots below ground; lilacs and roses are particularly prone to suckering.

Climbers

- From mid-spring, plant out new climbers into newly cultivated ground or in pots.
- Deadhead any climbers that repeat-flower (e.g. *Clematis* 'Alpine', *C.* 'Louise Rowe' and *C.* 'Carnaby') to provide you with a second flush later in the season.

- Prune any large-flowering clematis (e.g. *Clematis* 'Jackmanii', *C.* 'Nelly Moser' and *C.* 'Niobe') that have become unruly. They have brittle stems, so make sure you tie in new shoots to prevent them from breaking in the wind.
- Cut back evergreens and deciduous climbers that flower on new wood.
- In late spring after they have flowered, prune any spring-flowering climbers that flower on old wood.

Roses

- If the ground is not frozen or waterlogged, you can finish planting bare-root roses while they are available.
- Prune, weed and then feed and mulch established roses.
- Prune any repeat-flowering climbers, shrubs, bush and miniature roses.
- Tie in new growth on climbing and rambling roses.

- Re-pot and top-dress containerized roses.
- Deal with outbreaks of aphids as soon as you see them using soapy solution organic or chemical controls, as you see fit.

Perennials

- Preempt tall-growing herbaceous perennials like delphiniums and Michaelmas daisies by staking them before they begin to grow.
- Split any clumps of overgrown ornamental grasses and other perennial plants.

Division of perennials

Use the prongs of two forks to divide clumps, then push the two handles together to separate them.

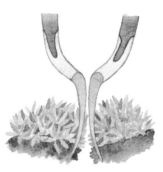

- When the weather begins to warm up, begin planting hardy perennials into prepared open ground or containers.
- If you did not cut back spent growth in autumn, remove dead material from herbaceous perennials to make room for new growth.
- If you have the time, remove any weak growth from the centre of crowded plants to promote stronger plants and better flowers.

Bulbs

- Plant dahlia tubers and other summer-flowering bulbs in late spring.
- Plant autumn-flowering *Nerine bowdenii*.
- Remove the spent flower-heads of daffodils and tulips to ensure energy is routed back to the bulb to promote the following year's blooms rather than be wasted on seed production. Always leave the foliage alone

until it yellows and then dies down naturally – leaves produce food that is ingested back into the bulb for the following year's display.
- In early to mid-spring, plant new snowdrops 'in the green'.
- Lift, divide and replant congested groups of snowdrops and winter aconites when the blooms have faded.
- Only cut the grass where bulbs have been flowering in late spring when the flowers and food-producing foliage have begun to die back.
- Begin to feed any summer bulbs whose foliage has begun to appear.

Annuals and biennials

- Sow seed of hardy annuals outside in their final growing positions as soon as the soil has warmed up.
- In late spring, sow the seed of hardy biennials in a seedbed outside, ready for the following spring.
- Plant out sweet pea seedlings sown the previous autumn.
- In early spring, sow half-hardy annuals under glass in the greenhouse to give them a head start.
- In mid-spring, start hardening off half-hardy annuals in a cold frame, making sure they are protected from any frosts.
- Plant out half-hardy annuals when all fear of late frosts has passed.
- Revive any over-wintered fuchsias and geraniums by plunging their pots into water and then pruning them back into shape.

Lawns and meadows

- Thoroughly prepare the ground for a new lawn by digging the area over, weeding and raking it out into as fine a tilth as possible before sowing seed or laying turf from mid-spring onwards.
- In mid-spring, repair any damaged patches within the lawn.
- After raking the area over, re-seed worn or bare patches.

Once mature, ponds require regular maintenance if you are to keep them in peak condition. Achieving that fine balance between natural environment and overgrown soup requires an investment of time, patience and money, but is very rewarding.

- In mid-spring, lightly scarify (rake to remove build-ups of thatch) and apply a general fertilizer, or if you prefer, weed and feed. The organic alternative is to lift weeds by hand using a long, sharp knife.
- Begin mowing established lawns as soon as they start to grow; make sure the lawnmower's blades are not set too low. Set the blades to about 2.5cm (1in) high, gradually lowering as the season progresses to 12mm (½in).
- Do not mow summer-flowering meadows after mid-spring.

The water garden

- In mid-spring, clear the blanket weed from garden ponds and thin out any overgrown oxygenators.
- Thin overgrown clumps of water lilies and remove some of the larger leaves.

- In late spring, clean out neglected or overgrown dirty ponds and pools.
- Lift and divide all aquatic and bog plants as necessary.
- In late spring, prepare planting pockets and begin planting aquatic marginals and bog plants.
- In late spring, on hot days, water the bog garden if you have one, to keep it moist.
- As the water temperature increases, give aquatic plants a boost with a high-phosphate fertilizer.

Fruit, vegetables and herbs

- In early spring, speed up the natural warming of the soil by covering the area you will be planting up with a layer of plastic film, fleece or cloches.

- Once the soil has warmed up (mid- to late spring), you can begin sowing vegetable seeds into moist ground.
- Sow vegetable seeds in succession to ensure a continuous supply of vegetables.
- Put up cane supports for peas and climbing beans.
- Force rhubarb and chicory.
- Sow tomato seeds in a greenhouse or even on a warm, bright windowsill.
- In late spring, plant up asparagus crowns, onion sets and shallots.
- Come late spring, plant out main crop potatoes before it is too late.
- Take care to protect early fruit blossoms from late frost.
- In mid- to late spring, plant out strawberries.
- Plant out container-grown herbs
- Sow the seed of perennial herbs.

SUMMER

Warm sun, plentiful bloom, sublime scents, buzzing bees, vegetables fit to bursting and long balmy evenings – summer is the time of year when gardeners can sit back and enjoy the fruits of their labour. However, this does not mean the gardener can become complacent. Although the heavier jobs are at an end, there is still plenty to do in your role as caretaker: feeding, watering and supporting plants, along with keeping an eye out for pests, weeds and diseases. While you are enjoying your garden, make sure you monitor it closely – not too hard a task for the keen gardener at home.

Trees and shrubs

• Prune late spring- and early summer-flowering shrubs after they have bloomed, thinning out any weak flowering shoots and cutting old, unproductive stems down to the base. These include lilac, deutzia, weigela, spirea and philadelphus.
• Begin trimming evergreen and coniferous hedges and topiary in early summer.
• In late summer, trim deciduous hedges.
• Watch out for suckers rising from the base of trees and shrubs and remove them as soon as they appear.
• Cut out the unwanted branches of any trees, but primarily shrubs that may be losing their variegation, in order to stop them from reverting to plain green.
• In early summer, take softwood cuttings of hardy fuchsia.
• From midsummer, take semi-hardwood cuttings of shrubs that are getting past their best, such as cistus and deutzia, and in order to increase your numbers of hydrangea, escallonia, euonymous, ceanothus, spirea and hypericum.
• In dry or windy weather, water newly planted trees very well, giving them more than you may think they need.

TAKING CUTTINGS

Cuttings are a great way to increase your plant numbers, replace worn out plants and provide you with plants to swap with friends. Some plants can be propagated from leaf and root cuttings, stem cuttings are the easiest type of cuttings. Not only are they easy but they are quick and guarantee an exact replica of the parent plant. Though the propagation techniques vary slightly depending upon what type of cutting you are taking and the time of year, always put cuttings straight into a plastic bag when they've been clipped from the plant to avoid them losing too much water.

Softwood cuttings are taken in late spring and early summer from the new soft growth of a plant. They're best taken first thing in the day before the plants have had a chance to lose water in the heat of the day. Cut growing tips about 15cm (6in) long, putting cuttings straight into a plastic bag. Once you've taken them inside or into the potting shed (should you be so lucky to have one!) take off the bottom few leaves and trim the cutting just below a leaf joint. Dip the cutting in water then hormone rooting powder, then poke the cutting into a pot filled with multi-purpose compost (mixed with sharp sand and/or vermiculite if you prefer) so that at least 5cm (2in) of the cutting is below the surface. Water your pot then slip a polythene bag over the top held in position with an elastic band (this will further prevent water loss and act as a miniature greenhouse) and put it on a window sill or in the greenhouse, where it will get plenty of sunlight. You'll know when the cutting has rooted by signs of new growth. Pot your rooted cuttings on into bigger pots at this stage, taking care not to damage the new roots. Surprisingly good results can be obtained by putting cuttings in a jar or container full of water. Place a piece of netting over the top of the jar before putting the stems in to keep the them separate. Plants suitable for this method include fuchsia, philadelphus, hebe, geranium, wisteria, choisia, achillea, campanula and delphinium.

Semi-ripe cuttings are taken towards the end of the summer when the shoots are beginning to ripen. Use the current year's growth for best results. They are treated in exactly the same way as softwood cuttings, the only difference being in the time of year they are taken. Semi-ripe cuttings will take longer to root than softwood cuttings, and new growth will probably not show until the following spring when your new plants can be potted on. Do not panic if your deciduous plants loose the few leaves they have over the winter; they haven't died, but have simply succumbed to the time of year. Suitable plants for this process include annual geraniums (pelargoniums), photinia, skimmia, lavender, rosemary, holly, choisya and most deciduous shrubs.

- Remove any dead, damaged or diseased stems from evergreens.
- Prune deciduous trees if you think they have outgrown their allotted space, and trim pleached deciduous trees in order to train them into shape.
- In late summer, order trees and shrubs required for winter planting.

Climbers

- Finish planting container-grown climbers by early summer.
- Water and deadhead plants throughout the summer, mulching wall-trained shrubs and climbers well in order to help them retain this moisture.
- Tie in new shoots to their supports in order to avoid damage.
- After they have finished flowering, prune back unruly plants that flower in summer on old wood. This will give them an opportunity to produce new stems before winter sets in.
- In late summer, carry out the first stage of pruning on wisteria. Prune the current year's growth back to the first five leaves to keep your plant neat and promote flowering.
- Take softwood cuttings in midsummer.

Roses

- If you have any gaps in your rose bed, plant containerized roses now. Dig in some well-rotted manure when you plant, and a sprinkling of bonemeal, then keep the new additions well watered.
- Remove any suckers from the base of plants so that energy is not wasted.
- Keep a close eye out for aphids, and treat any other pests and diseases you come across before they take hold.
- Give roses a good feed while they are flowering, be it their first or second flush.
- Deadhead the blooms of roses as soon as they have finished in order to encourage new growth and perhaps a second flush of blooms later in the year.

- In late summer, order bare-root plants for late autumn.
- In late summer, prune rambling roses and any old roses after they have flowered in order to give new shoots time to mature before autumn and winter set in.

Perennials

- Cut back early flowering perennials such as aquilegia and dorinicum after blooming to about 15cm (6in) if you want to discourage them from self-seeding
- In early summer, cut back the old flower stems of *Euphorbia characias* to the ground. New stems will quickly fill the void.
- Lift and divide primroses and polyanthus after flowering, planting them in a shady spot to protect them through the summer in deep, fertile, humus-rich soil.
- Lift and divide bearded iris in early summer after they have bloomed.
- Early summer is also the time to finish sowing the seed of hardy perennials outdoors for flowering the following year.
- Continue to deadhead and remove any ailing yellow foliage throughout the summer.
- Water plants in containers daily in hot or windy weather.
- Late summer gives rise to mildew (asters are particularly susceptible). Water all plants well at ground level before they flower in order to prevent it from occurring.
- Collect the seed from any herbaceous perennials you want to increase stocks of.
- Take softwood cuttings of plants you are worried about losing through the winter, such as penstemons and diascias.

Bulbs

- Continue to leave the foliage of bulbs to die down naturally. Only remove this foliage after a minimum of six weeks after flowering.
- In late summer, order bulbs for an autumn planting session.

Routine jobs for summer

- In early summer, plant up containers to give you a good summer display. Incorporate a slow-release fertilizer to negate the need for a weekly feed, and incorporate 'swell gel' (a water-retaining agent designed for just this purpose) into the compost to cut down on watering.

- In periods of particularly hot, dry weather, make sure you water any plants that have recently been planted or that are still in the early stages of growth (particularly trees and shrubs planted over the winter or spring). They will not yet have built up a sufficient root system to collect enough water to sustain top growth and will need your help with a regular, sometimes daily, dowse with the hose.

- Deadhead all your plants once blooms are past their best in order to encourage new buds and blooms.

- Watch out for greenfly and aphids. A spray of soapy water will help keep them in check.

- If you did not get around to mulching borders in the spring, make sure you do it now in order to conserve water in the ground.

- Hoe borders and beds regularly to cut down on weeds.

- Check all the supports and ties on plants and replace broken ones regularly before the plant itself becomes damaged.

- Plant out any young dahlia plants you have raised from cuttings or seed.
- In midsummer, plant any autumn-flowering bulbs (crocuses, *Sternbergia lutea* and colchicums).
- Deadhead blooms unless you are saving the seed.
- If you want to ensure a return visit, lift, dry and then store tulip bulbs once the foliage has died down, ready for replanting in late autumn.
- Divide and replant any overcrowded clumps of bulbs when they have finished blooming.
- Water summer-flowering bulbs well, giving them a regular feed.
- Watch out for the appearance of autumn-flowering bulbs planted in the lawn and, once they have arrived, stop mowing.
- Late summer brings dahlias into bloom. Feed them regularly while they flower.

Annuals

- If you sow a second batch of annuals in early summer, once the first sowings are past their best, they can be easily replaced.
- If you did not sow biennial seeds in a nursery bed in late spring, do so in early summer; this is your last opportunity for blooms the following year.
- When any chance of a late frost has passed, plant out pelargoniums (annual geraniums) as summer bedding.
- If you are buying bedding plants, choose strong healthy plants with bright green leaves, only planting them out when all risk of a late frost is over.
- Deadhead annuals regularly to divert energy into producing new blooms rather than seed, ensuring a long flowering season.
- Pick sweet peas each week to promote lots of flower. Do not allow any blooms to set seed or bloom quantities will be reduced.
- In late summer, sow pansies and violets for winter and spring flowering.

- Late summer is the time to take cuttings from annual pelargoniums in order to increase your stocks for the following year.
- At the end of the summer season, collect the seed of annuals and store them for sowing the following year.

A lawn seat is a practical and economical way of increasing seating in your garden. It does not just invite you to sit down and admire the view, but is a great talking point, too.

Lawns

- After blooming, give a spring-flowering meadow its first cut.
- Feed the lawn with a summer lawn fertilizer to keep it in mint condition.
- In dry weather, raise the height of the mower's blade and remove the collecting box; the clippings can be used as a mulch.
- Water the lawn regularly during hot weather if it is important to you to keep it green. Remember that an established lawn will recover from sun scorch if you want to conserve water.
- Dig over and prepare any areas of the lawn you want to seed the following year.

The water garden

- If you have not already given your water garden a spring clean, clean it out now, lifting and dividing water lilies and other aquatic plants and adding aquatics and marginals where required.
- Plant aquatic and marginals in midsummer.
- Do not plant deep-water plants until late summer.
- Clear blanket weed from ponds.
- Feed water lilies in midsummer.
- Remember to keep the water topped up in hot weather.
- Thin out the foliage of water lilies if they begin to get overcrowded and keep oxygenating plants in check, too.
- If aphids attack water lilies, spray them off with a water jet.
- Keep water clear of algae before large masses form, removing it with a rake.

Fruit, vegetables and herbs

- In early summer, earth up potatoes and stake and tie-in tomatoes.
- Train climbing vegetables in midsummer.
- Provide support to any branches that are becoming particularly heavy with their burden of fruit.
- Plant new strawberry runners, should you need to, early in the season.
- Thin out the fruitlets on fruit trees if they are too plentiful.
- Prune summer-fruiting raspberries and train in new canes.
- Continue sowing vegetables in small batches to enjoy a succession of cropping.
- Pick soft fruit and vegetables regularly.
- Unless you incorporated a slow-release fertilizer in the spring, make sure you feed vegetables regularly.
- Towards the end of the summer, harvest and store vegetables and fruit for consumption throughout the winter.
- Lift and dry onions in late summer.

AUTUMN

During autumn, clouds hang low in the sky and morning mists glide skywards to meet them, and colours in the garden are warmer and generally more restful – browns, ochre, reds and yellows are mellow proof that the garden is approaching its winter retreat. Enjoying the seasonal flux is an undeniable pleasure, but the garden is certainly losing its momentum at this time of year. Autumn offers the final window to carry out those improvements you have been planning and to complete the garden chores you have been putting off. In order to improve your space for the following year, put your garden to bed properly while you still can. Think about what you can do to prepare for the coming winter and ensuing spring.

Taking hardwood cuttings

- Take hardwood cuttings from hard, mature wood in late autumn to winter. Take cuttings 15cm (6in) long, removing the lower leaves of evergreens.
- Deciduous plants will be leafless by now but treat them in the same way as cuttings taken earlier in the year, cutting the stem at an angle just above a bud.
- Make a deep V-shaped trench in the soil and backfill it with some sharp sand (available from builders' merchants).
- Set the cuttings about 10cm (4in) apart, leaning them against the side of the trench.
- Backfill with earth so that about 2.5cm (1in) is above ground, then leave them undisturbed for at least a year.
- The back of the border or beside the shed out of sight is an ideal place for this purpose. Shrubs suitable for this method include cornus, spirea, roses and viburnum.

Trees and shrubs

- Take hardwood cuttings from deciduous shrubs that have lost their leaves, before the soil gets too cold. These include forsythia, kerria, philadelphus and weigela.
- Trees and shrubs go into the dormant season now, so it is the perfect time to plant new additions.
- Protect tender or half-hardy woody plants with fleece, straw or conifer branches.
- Check the stakes and ties of your trees.
- Carry out annual, formative (training) and renovation pruning of deciduous trees and hedges. Also remove any dead, damaged or diseased wood from trees and shrubs.
- If you want to move any trees and shrubs from one spot to another in your garden, now is a good time to transplant them.
- Feed half-hardy shrubs with sulphate of potash, which helps ripen wood and make it less prone to frost damage and disease.
- Plant conifers and evergreens while the ground is still warm.
- Bring container-grown fuchsias, hydrangeas and other frost-tender plants into the greenhouse or shed to protect them throughout the winter.

Climbers

- Plant climbers into prepared, fertilized soil where there has been a generous addition of organic matter or compost.
- Repot and/or top-dress any plants in containers.
- Make sure that all climbers are well supported and tied in, replacing any ties where necessary.
- Layer climbers to increase their numbers.
- Gather the ripe seeds of clematis to sow them in the cold frame later in autumn.

Roses

- Feed roses with sulphate of potash to help ripen the wood, making them less prone to frost damage and disease.
- Continue to deadhead roses for as long as they are flowering.
- In mid-autumn, cut back shrub roses by about a third to make them less susceptible to winter winds that could cause them to rock, thereby damaging their roots. You can use the clippings as hardwood cuttings.
- Plant bare-root roses as soon as they become available.
- Check any stakes and ties that are supporting the roses.

Perennials

- Now is the best time to plant containerized perennials, allowing plants plenty of time to get their roots down while the ground is still warm.
- Deadhead any plants that would not contribute to the garden's winter outline. Add the chopped up material to the compost heap.
- When a plant has finished flowering, cut back the head and remove any supports, stakes or unsightly plant debris.
- In all but the coldest areas, cut hardy plants back to the base when they begin to look past their best.
- Lift, split and divide congested clumps of established herbaceous perennials, replanting them where there are appropriate gaps in your borders. Hardy geraniums and hostas are usually good candidates for this treatment.
- Lift tender plants that would not survive the winter and store them in a shed or greenhouse.
- Collect seeds as they continue to ripen, keeping them in labelled envelopes until you are ready to sow them.

Bulbs

- Plant spring-flowering bulbs in prepared ground and/or containers and prepared bulbs for forcing.
- After the first frost has knocked them back, lift, dry out and then store dahlia tubers and any other tender perennials.
- Plant bulb irises for late winter and early

PLANTING A TREE

Planting trees is good for the soul and a lovely thing to do at this time of year. You are investing in the future of a space, providing habitats for wildlife and contributing to the greening up of your locality. As such, take pleasure in the preparation, providing the tree with the best conditions you can, so that it will thrive, not just survive. Make sure you choose a tree that will be in scale with your garden, considering the total area it will cover when mature.

1 Water the tree in its container before you start work to ensure that the roots are moist.
2 On digging a planting hole, ensure that the hole is at least 60cm (2ft) in diameter and at least 50cm (20in) deep, removing any weeds that you might encounter and loosening the soil in the bottom of the hole.
3 Once you have removed the topsoil, punch the sides of the hole with a garden fork to enable the tree roots to penetrate into the ground.
4 Hammer a stake into the ground before you plant, slightly off-centre and on the windward side.
5 Mix up some topsoil with rotted organic matter or garden compost. (If you are

planting in spring, mixing in a handful of slow-release fertilizer is a good idea to give the tree some added energy.)

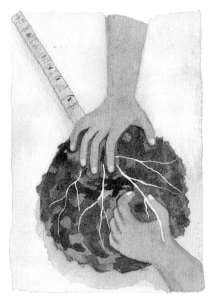

6 Remove the tree from its pot, teasing out any overly pot-bound roots.
7 Backfill the planting hole with soil to a level where the tree will sit at the correct planting depth. The tree should be at the same level in the ground as it was in the pot. If you are unsure of this depth, a dark line near the base of the stem will indicate it.
8 Place the tree in the ground and then backfill with top soil/organic matter mix, firming it down in stages in order to knock out any air holes.
9 After tying the tree to the stake with an adjustable tie, lightly fork over the whole area and then water in well.
10 Use a mulch to lock in moisture and keep weeds down, and until the tree is completely established, keep the surrounding area weed- and grass-free.

In autumn, you can buy trees and shrubs in three forms:

Containerized trees and shrubs are grown and supplied by the nursery in containers. They are available and can be planted all year round.

Root-balled trees and shrubs are grown in the field until they are lifted for transplanting in autumn and winter when the trees are dormant. The soil in which they were growing is left intact around the roots, and this root ball is then encased in hessian and/or a wire basket to keep it secure. These are left on the tree when replanted.

Bare-root trees and shrubs are grown in the open ground until they are lifted in autumn and winter when they are dormant. They are transported without soil around the roots, so they need to be planted immediately on receipt. Although they are not as reliable as containerized or root-balled plants, they are sold at bargain prices, costing significantly less if you are buying several plants, perhaps for a hedge.

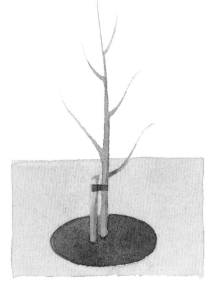

spring flowering and lily bulbs for the following summer as soon as they become available.

● In mid-autumn, protect tender bulbs with a thick layer of mulch or straw.

● Tulips are one of the last bulbs to be planted; make sure you have them all in the ground before the end of autumn.

Annuals and biennials

● Clear away any annuals and biennials that have finished flowering.

● Plant out early sown biennials in the open ground where they are to flower.

● Sow hardy annuals in the open ground, thinning and then transplanting them later in the season.

● Sow sweet pea seeds in a sheltered, sunny spot or cold frame in order to get a head start the following spring.

● Collect seed from late-flowering annuals and biennials.

● Fill gaps in borders or containers with winter-flowering pansies, wallflowers, forget-me-nots and bellis daisies as soon as they become available.

● Overwinter half-hardy perennials treated as annuals before the first serious frosts. Pots of fuchsia and pelargoniums can be stored in pots on the windowsill if you do not have a greenhouse.

The water garden

● Remove all dead and dying growth, and the seedpods from invasive plants to stop them from reproducing.

● Keep your pond free of leaves by covering it with a net.

● In mid-autumn, protect the crowns of tender plants such as gunnera by folding its own dead foliage over the crown, or by covering it with a layer of straw.

A water feature, be it informal or, as seen here, formal, not only allows you more growing opportunities, but is also the quickest way to invite wildlife into your garden.

MULCH

A mulch is a layer of material spread approximately 5–10cm (2–4in) deep over the surface of the ground between and around plants. Though not essential, mulch is highly advisable as a labour-saving, soil-improving material on many levels. It keeps the soil warm to promote root growth, locking moisture into the ground by slowing down the evaporation of water. An organic mulch protects plant roots from the excessive cold of frost or snow, eventually rotting down and adding nutrients to the soil. A thick layer of mulch also acts as a weed suppressant while framing and highlighting the qualities of the plants you want to cultivate.

Mulches need to be topped up regularly because even an inorganic mulch will sink into the soil over time. Add another layer whenever the mulch starts to run thin.

Organic mulches include garden compost, leaf mould, chipped bark, mushroom compost, cocoa shells, multi-purpose compost and manure.

Inorganic mulches range from the practical but not very attractive carpet, plastic sheet and weed-proof membrane (perhaps best kept to the allotment and vegetable garden rather than the open border unless they are disguised with a layer of organic mulch on top) to attractive gravel, cobbles and chipped slate or shale.

For the keen gardener, a scrap of land in town provides the perfect opportunity to grow an eclectic range of both ornamental and productive plants, such as these colourful flowers and vegetables growing side by side.

• Move tender, floating plants into a frost-free area.

• Get your pump serviced to keep it in mint condition and overhaul your fountains and filters.

• Thin out oxygenating plants in early autumn.

• Divide and then transplant established clumps of aquatic, marginal and bog plants in order to prevent overcrowding.

Lawns

• Cut back spring- and summer-flowering meadows.

• Apply an autumn feed to the lawn, particularly if it has had heavy use over the summer.

• Scarify (rake with a spring-tined rake) the lawn to remove moss and dead clippings, spike it with a fork, and then top dress (spread) with a thin layer of multi-purpose compost or sand to get it into shape for the following year.

• In mild areas, a new lawn can be established in early autumn either from seed or ready-made turf.

• Keep the lawn clear of leaves that could block out light and damage it.

Fruit, vegetables and herbs

• Lift and pot up mature herbs for winter use indoors.

• In early autumn, cut back shrubby herbs.

• In early autumn, plant winter salad vegetables and oriental brassicas under cover and stake and earth up winter brassicas where necessary.

• Plant tree, bush and cane fruits in late autumn.

• Prune fan-trained peaches and nectarines after they have fruited.

• Sow alpine strawberries.

• Lots of vegetables will be ready to harvest now, including marrows, onions and sweetcorn. Continue to pick beans and peas until they are spent.

Routine jobs for autumn

• Tidy up borders by cutting back those stems and flowerheads that add nothing to the silhouettes of winter, and by removing annuals that have finished flowering.

• Keep the garden clear of fallen leaves. Gather them up and add them to the compost heap.

• Clear containers of summer bedding displays to make room for winter ones.

• Make plans for the following year, digging over any new beds you have decided upon and within beds that are to be given an overhaul. This is particularly useful in clay soils as winter frosts will help to break up the ground.

• Open greenhouse windows to allow air to circulate, thereby preventing the build-up of disease.

• Re-firm soil around plants that has been loosened by wind and/or rain.

• Mulch all planted areas to protect plants from the cold and to retain moisture and warmth in the ground for as long as possible.

• Turn over the compost heap and add this compost to the ground as a soil improver or as a mulch to provide winter protection to more tender plants.

• Put out bird feeders and water now to encourage regular visits. Come spring, birds will return the favour by feasting upon pests in your garden.

WINTER

Take time out to think about how your garden has performed for you this year, and how it can be improved for the following year. Although most of your plants are hibernating below ground at this time of year, it is a great time to carry out any hard landscaping you require: path building, new terraces and carpentry, too. Ground can be dug over (weather permitting) to create new beds, ready for you to plant up come spring. On rainy days, take advantage of the weather to look through gardening catalogues – the perfect introduction and inspiration for seeds, new plant varieties and new tools to invest in for the coming year.

Fertilizer

Plants need several nutrients in soil in order to thrive, but only three need to be added to the soil regularly to promote healthy plant growth: nitrogen, phosphorus and potassium. All of these can be found in the concentrated organic fertilizer fish, blood and bone that will slowly release these nutrients into the ground.

Nitrogen (N) promotes the vigorous growth of foliage. However, as with all fertilizers, do not get too 'plant-food-happy'; too much nitrogen can produce lots of foliage to the detriment of flowers and too much vigorous growth can result in sappy plants that are more attractive to pests and susceptible to disease. Add a high-nitrogen fertilizer if a plant's leaves appear pale green or yellow, if a plant looks weak or stunted. Lawns will benefit from a regular nitrogen feed, too. If you are looking for a nitrogen-only feed, it can be found as dried blood.

Phosphorus (P) or phosphates ensure strong root growth. A deficiency is marked by the leaves of a plant generally looking unhealthy, turning a dull bluish-green and by poor root

LAYERING SHRUBS AND CLIMBERS

Layering is a cheap and simple way of producing new plants by covering an individual stem with soil in order to encourage it to produce roots while it is still attached to the parent plant. Once rooted, the new plant is simply cut away from the parent. This is a very effective technique to use with climbers and where you have a large wall or fence to cover on a low budget.

The easiest method of layering is known as 'simple layering' and is best carried out in winter. Choose a vigorous stem of the current year's growth, ensuring that it is flexible enough to be brought down to soil level without damage. Make a shallow slanted cut on the underside of the stem to be layered, then peg it into the ground using a U-shaped piece of well-covered wire (coat hangers are ideal for this purpose). Tie the end of the shoot to a vertical cane pushed into the ground to support it. By the following autumn, the new plant should have rooted and can be cut from the parent plant and replanted elsewhere. This method can be expanded to create a 'serpentine layer' suitable for very pliable stems on plants such as clematis. One long shoot is pegged at intervals, leaving intermittent lengths of stem exposed to leaf up, thereby producing several individual plants.

growth. These effects often occur in very waterlogged or very acid soil. Bone meal is a good source of phosphorus.

Potassium (K) improves the flowers and fruit of a plant. Poor quantities of flowers and fruit, combined with small size, can indicate a potassium deficiency in a plant. The leaves upon the plant may turn yellow or brown around the edges, sometimes even rolling in on themselves. Sulphate of potash is a good source of potassium.

Trees and shrubs

• Continue to prune trees and shrubs if they need to be cut back (broken limbs, crossing branches where disease could easily enter, overhanging branches) while the plants are dormant.
• Winter is a good time to layer shrubs to increase their numbers.
• Plant container-grown, deciduous, bare-root and root-balled trees and shrubs, provided the ground is not frozen. Stake tall specimens for support.

• In areas exposed to frost or chilling coastal winds, protect the buds of rhododendrons and azaleas with sacking or horticultural fleece. Uncover on still, sunny days and as the weather begins to warm up.
• Start coppicing and pollarding any trees and shrubs that require it in late winter.

Climbers

• Layer climbers in order to produce more plants for spring.
• Plant out container-grown plants where required, weather permitting.
• In early winter, prune ornamental vines (*Vitis vinifera* 'Purpurea', *Vitis coignetiae*) to keep them tidy.
• Carry out the second stage of pruning wisteria in midwinter.
• Keep checking supports and ties to ensure climbers are well supported in case of strong winds.
• Prune late-flowering hybrid clematis back to 22–25cm (9–10in) from the ground. Feed them with a general slow-release fertilizer and mulch the plants well.

• If pruning of deciduous climbers is required, carry it out now while the plants are dormant.

Roses

• Plant new bushes and transplant established ones into well-prepared ground, weather permitting.

• In late winter, tie in the shoots of climbers and rambling roses that could be damaged by strong winds.

Perennials

• Continue to remove and store any untidy looking plant supports, removing plant debris around them.

• If you are a keen flower arranger, place cloches over *Helleborus niger* to lengthen their stems and keep the flowers clean.

• Prepare beds for spring planting, digging them over and incorporating plenty of organic matter and fertilizer.

Bulbs

• Start off dahlia tubers undercover in a greenhouse to get a head start.

• Check stored tender bulbs, corms and tubers occasionally for any signs of rot. Destroy any badly affected bulbs and dust the rest over with a fungicide to ensure that the rot does not spread.

• As the foliage of early spring bulbs begins to appear, lightly prick the soil around the leaves in order to aerate it.

• Give bulbs beginning to push through the soil a light sprinkling of general-purpose fertilizer.

Annuals and biennials

• Plan the following year's annual scheme by browsing through seed catalogues and ordering your choices. As it arrives, file the envelopes in sowing order to make life easier.

• Protect autumn-sown sweet peas growing in coldframes by covering the glass with some matting or pieces of old carpet during heavy frost.

• Dig over the areas you will be planting with annuals in preparation for spring.

• If you have a heated greenhouse, start growing slow-growing annuals such as begonias and lobelias.

Lawns

• Keep off the lawn after a heavy frost; walking on it can cause damage.

• Brush off any leaves and worm casts that develop but keep off the lawn if it is very wet or frosty.

• Get your mower serviced, and sharpen the blades in readiness for spring.

• Prepare areas for a new lawn and lay turf in early winter, weather permitting. If it is too cold, prepare areas to be grassed over in preparation for spring.

The water garden

• Keep your pond free of ice (which can be harmful to fish) by installing a pool heater or floating a plastic ball on the water's surface so that the whole surface cannot freeze over completely. This will create a breather hole so that fish do not suffocate.

• Remove snow from the surface of ice or plants may die from lack of light.

• Remove the water pump and get it serviced.

Fruit, vegetables and herbs

• Prune fruit trees while they are dormant.

• Plan the following year's crop rotation.

• Order seeds of vegetables and herbs from seed catalogues.

• Dig over and apply manure to empty beds, preparing them for spring sowing.

• In late winter, set up seed potatoes to sprout indoors.

• Continue to plant tree, bush and cane fruit.

Routine jobs for winter

• Plan any changes to your garden, marking out new structures on the garden with string, sand or spray line (aerosol spray paint especially for this purpose is available from garden centres and builders' yards), then live with them for a while to ensure that you are happy with their positioning.

• Continue to collect fallen leaves and to tidy up borders when plants are past their best.

• Dig spaces in existing beds over or create completely new beds, incorporating plenty of manure, compost or other organic matter. Remember: if you find it difficult to get your fork into the ground, what chance has a plant got – keep persevering!

• Check boundary fences, making any necessary repairs and/or painting them with preservative while deciduous climbers have cleared your way to them.

• Go through your shed, throwing away anything that is damaged, useless or needs replacing. Your tools with benefit from a quick clean down. Sharpen and oil them as you go.

• Wash out propagators, seed trays and pots so that they are ready to use when spring arrives.

• Check over the plant labels in your beds, replacing any that have broken or faded.

• Buy in quantities of fertilizer, compost, twine, wire, vine eyes and so on. This will ensure that you are ready for action when spring finally kicks off.

SOURCES and SUPPLIERS

Reclaimed Timber

Ashwell Recycling Co Ltd
Wick Place
Brentwood Road
Buphan, Upminster
Essex NG32 3PB
www.ashwellrecycling.com

Lassco Flooring
Maltby Street
Bermondsey
London SE1 3PA
www.lassco.co.uk/flooring

General Supplies

Travis Perkins Trading
   Company
Head Office
Lodge Way House
Lodge Way
Harleston Road
Northampton NN5 7UG
www.travisperkins.co.uk

Bricks

Freshfield Lane Brickworks
Danehill
Haywards Heath
West Sussex RH17 7HH
www.flb.uk.com

Ibstock Brick Ltd
Leybrook Works
Goose Green
Thakeham
Pulborough
West Sussex RH20 2LW
www.ibstock.co.uk

Paving Materials

Stonemarket Ltd
Oxford Road
Ryton on Dunsmore
Warwickshire CV8 3EJ
www.stonemarket.co.uk

Marshalls
Landscape House
Premier Way
Lowfields Business Park
Elland HX5 9HT
www.marshalls.co.uk/
   transform

Garden Furniture

Gaze Burvill
Redloh House
2 Michael Road
London SW6 2AD
www.gazeburvill.com

Twelve Limited
19 Barn Street
Stoke Newington
London N16 0JT
www.twelvelimited.com

Steel Water Features and Ornaments

Designs in Stainless
Unit 2 Semley Business Park
Station Road
Semley
Near Shaftesbury
Dorset SP7 9AN
www.designs-in-
   stainless.co.uk

Garden Products

The Organic Gardening
   Catalogue
Riverdene Business Park
Molesey Road
Hersham
Surrey KT12 4RG
www.OrganicCatalog.com

Stone and Gravel

Stonell
Forstal House
Maidstone Road

Beltring
Paddock Wood
Kent TN12 6PY
www.stonell.com

CED
728 London Road
West Thurrock
Grays
Essex RM20 3LU
www.ced.ltd.uk

Specialist Aggregates
162 Cannock Road
Stafford ST17 0QJ
www.specialistaggregates.
   co.uk

Pots

Whichford Pottery
Whichford
Near Shipston-on-Stour
Warwickshire CV36 5PG
www.whichfordpottery.com

The Pot Company
Charolais House
Maynards Farm
A21 Lamberhurst Quarter
Kent TN3 8AL
www.thepotco.com

Plants

Tendercare Nurseries
Southlands Road
Denham
Middlesex UB9 4HD
www.tendercare.co.uk

Architectural Plants
Cooks Farm
Nuthurst
Horsham
West Sussex RH13 6LH
www.architecturalplants.com

Rickard's Hardy Ferns
Kyre Park
Kyre
Tenbury Wells
Worcestershire WR15 8RP
Tel: 01885 410282

The Palm Centre
Ham Central Nursery
Ham Street
Ham
Richmond
Surrey TW10 7AH
www.palmcentre.co.uk

The Beth Chatto Gardens
Elmstead Market
Colchester
Essex CO7 7DB
www.bethchatto.co.uk

Bulbs

Jacques Amand
   International
The Nurseries
Clamp Hill
Stanmore
Middlesex HA7 3JS
www.jacquesamand.
   co.uk
Tel: 020 84207110

Water Plants and Equipment

Stapeley Water Gardens
London Road
Stapeley
Nantwich
Cheshire CW5 7LH
www.stapeleywatergardens.
   com

Hammocks

The Mexican Hammock
   Company
42 Beauchamp Road
Bristol BS7 8LQ
www.hammocks.co.uk

Live Willow

Somerset Levels Basket &
   Craft Centre Ltd
Lyng Road
Burrowbridge
Bridgwater
Somerset TA7 0SG
www.somersetlevels.co.uk

Hurdles

English Hurdle
Curload
Stoke St Gregory
Taunton
Somerset TA3 6JD
www.hurdle.co.uk

Further Reading

The RHS Plant Finder
Dorling Kindersley
Updated annually

*The RHS Encylopedia
   of Trees and Shrubs*
Dorling Kindersley
ISBN 0751303038

*The RHS Encylopedia
   of Gardening*
Dorling Kindersley
ISBN 1405303530

External Works
The Endat Group Ltd
ISBN 0953611159

Hardscape
David and Charles
ISBN 0715310089

The Essential Garden Book
Conran Octopus
ISBN 1850299196

Gardens Are for People
University of California
   Press
ISBN 0520201205

ACKNOWLEDGEMENTS

I would like to thank all the owners of the gardens included in this book, without whose help it would never have existed – Trevor Hotz, Alison Miles, Ruth and Mark Hodierne, Jonathan Lubert and Greg, James and Shelagh Clarke, Colleen Boxall, Jim Archer, Gill Freedman, Kate and Guiseppe Monuli, and Pippa South. I'd also like to thank Pippa Rubinstein and Judith Robertson for their patient and encouraging guidance on the writing of this book and Nicky Cooney for her wonderful illustrations. Steve Wooster's photography and generosity has been amazing – thank you. Dr C Whitehouse at the RHS Advisory Service has been fantastically helpful, too. Finally I'd like to thank all my family and friends for their constant support, advice and enthusiasm even through the most difficult of times – you know who you are. But most notably I'd like to thank Jules not only for his patience, for keeping my spirits up and putting a smile on my face, but also for lugging lots of printouts home for me to identify. Oh, and also thank you to our new baby, for not (so far!) coming early and so letting me finish this book!